RICHISTAN

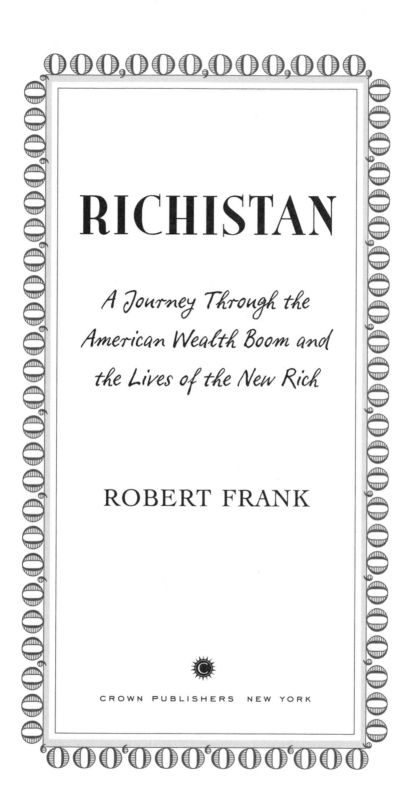

RICHISTAN

A Journey Through the
American Wealth Boom and
the Lives of the New Rich

ROBERT FRANK

CROWN PUBLISHERS   NEW YORK

Library of Congress Cataloging-in-Publication Data
Frank, Robert L.
Richistan : a journey through the American wealth boom
and the lives of the new rich / Robert L. Frank.—1st ed.
Includes bibliographical references and index.
1. Wealth—United States. 2. Rich people—United States.
3. Millionaires—United States. I. Title.
HC110.W4F73   2007
305.5'2340973—dc22   2006101942

ISBN 978-0-307-33926-3

Printed in the United States of America

DESIGN BY BARBARA STURMAN

10 9 8 7 6 5 4 3 2 1

First Edition

To Rebecca

Contents

RICHISTAN

Introduction

THE BIRTH OF
A NATION

This book began with the discovery of a single, remarkable statistic.

In 2003, while writing a routine article about Wall Street bonuses, I stumbled onto a chart from the Federal Reserve Board. It showed that the number of millionaire households had more than doubled since 1995 to more than eight million.

Granted, a million dollars doesn't mean what it used to. But no matter how far up I looked on the wealth ladder—to households worth $10 million, $20 million, $50 million—all the populations were doubling.

Even more surprising was the fact that the United States was minting millionaires long after the tech bust, recession and terrorist attacks of 2001. The wealth boom, as the numbers showed, went far beyond the 20-something dot-commers in Silicon Valley and Wall Streeters in New York. It stretched across the country, to all age groups and to almost every industry. Never before had so many Americans become so rich, so quickly. The United States is now the world leader in producing millionaires—even if it lags behind China and India in other types of manufacturing. For the first time in history, we now have more millionaires than Europe.

MILLIONAIRE HOUSEHOLDS			
(in millions) based on 2004 dollars			
	1M	5M	10M	25M
1995	3.77	.55	.23	.05
1998	5.43	.86	.30	.06
2004	9.05	1.44	.53	.11

SOURCE: Federal Reserve Board Surveys of Consumer Finance

After seeing the Fed numbers, I started to wonder about all these rich people. Who were they? How did they get rich? How was money changing their lives? Most importantly, how were they changing life for the rest of us? Why, in an age of "millionaire" reality TV shows and wealth voyeurism, did we seem to know so little about what this group was *really* like?

To answer these questions, my editors agreed to a bold experiment. In 2003, I became the first reporter at *The Wall Street Journal* to focus full-time on the life and times of the New Rich. I immersed myself in their world, hanging around yacht marinas, slipping into charity balls, loitering in Ferrari dealerships and scoping out the Sotheby's and

Christie's auctions. I studied up on trust law, high-end investing and the latest trends in charitable giving. I grilled the top luxury realtors, jet brokers, party planners and resort managers. Mostly, I bothered rich people. I asked them endless questions and tried to get them to talk openly about their money and their lives. Surprisingly, many did. The resulting articles I wrote about this new culture of wealth proved surprisingly popular with readers.

This book began with that reporting. But its central premise—of a parallel country of the rich—took shape later, with a chance conversation at a yacht club. In 2004, I was walking along the docks of Ft. Lauderdale's Bahia Mar Marina during an annual yacht convention when I met up with a boat owner from Texas. As we stared out over the hundreds of megayachts lined up along the docks— most 150 feet or more, flying Caribbean flags emblazoned with fruit—he turned to me and said, "You look at all these boats and you'd think everyone's making loads of money. It's like it's a different country."

The words stuck with me. Today's rich had formed their own virtual country. They were, in fact, wealthier than most nations. By 2004, the richest 1 percent of Americans were earning about $1.35 trillion a year—greater than the total national incomes of France, Italy or Canada.

And with their huge numbers, they had built a self-contained world unto themselves, complete with their own health-care system (concierge doctors), travel network (Net Jets, destination clubs), separate economy (double-digit income gains and double-digit inflation), and language ("Who's your household manager?"). They didn't just hire gardening crews; they hired "personal arborists." The rich weren't just getting richer; they were becoming financial foreigners, creating their own country within a country, their own society within a society, and their economy within an economy.

They were creating Richistan.

As a former foreign correspondent, I set out to explore this new country. I spent 12 months traveling around and interviewing the most interesting Richistanis I could find—all worth $10 million or more. They are people you've never heard of, since so many of today's wealthy prefer to keep to themselves. And they have little in common with Donald Trump, Bill Gates, Warren Buffet and the other well-known Forbes 400 superstars we read so much about.

Along the way, I discovered a new culture of wealth that's vastly different from Old Money. I found Richistanis who have made vast fortunes from things we barely knew existed—like miniature ceramic villages. And I learned that the very *way* that people get rich is changing, driven by vast pools of money sloshing around the world.

I met a song-writing, jet-setting timber baron named Tim Blixseth who typifies the new breed of "workaholic wealthy" who can't stop building empires even after becoming billionaires. And I met a risk-loving entrepreneur named Pete Musser who lost his entire billion-dollar fortune in the stock market and is now plotting his comeback.

I attended a black-tie ball in Palm Beach, where a brash pool-toy magnate tried to climb to the top of blue-blood Society, only to come crashing down (literally) on Donald Trump's ballroom floor. I sat in on a meeting of a wealth peer group, a new kind of group therapy for millionaires who need help with their money troubles. And I spent a day at Rich Kids Camp, where the new silver spoon set learn how to manage all the money they're about to inherit.

I jumped aboard some of today's biggest yachts, to see how Richistanis are reinventing the notion of conspicuous consumption. I also looked at how that spending is "trickling down" to the rest of America, for better and worse. I met a Jewish Irishman in Texas who's giving away half his fortune to help fight poverty in Ethiopia and embodies a new brand of philanthropy. And I explored Richistan's politics through a group called the Gang of Four—four wealthy Coloradans who helped fund a Democratic takeover of the state legislature and have helped to usher in a new kind of progressive, rich man's politics.

Of course, Americans are conflicted about all this wealth. On the one hand, Richistanis represent all that's great about the American economy and the ability of just about anyone anywhere to become wealthy. Yet Richistan also symbolizes the huge gap that's opened up between the rich and everyone else. Even as the rich have grown more numerous, they have also become more financially and culturally removed from the rest of America. Richistan's success highlights Middle America's loss.

The purpose of my journey isn't to take sides in this debate. I haven't set out to condemn the rich, or to turn them into heroes. The best foreign correspondents seek to bring readers inside a country, to explore its people and places and explain them to the rest of the world. I have the same goal with *Richistan.*

The economist John Kenneth Galbraith once wrote that "Of all the classes, the wealthy are the most noticed and the least studied." That has never been more true than today. To understand inequality, we need to first understand Richistan and the people who live there.

So let's begin our journey with a quick tour.

Three Parts of a New Country

Before the late 1980s, the rich lived in a small, quiet enclave of like-minded people. They went to many of the same schools, belonged to the same clubs, had similar values and often married into each other's families. It was more like a village than a country. Breeding and pedigree mattered as much as bank accounts, and most Richistanis were born into their money, which usually flowed from oil, chemicals, steel, real estate and commodities.

New fortunes were rare, since the economy spread its gains far beyond Richistan, and the prevailing culture and politics of the time discouraged outsized wealth. When the first Forbes 400 list hit newstands in 1982, the richest man was a thrifty shipping magnate named Daniel Ludwig, who was worth $2 billion. After that, the roster was filled with turn-of-the-century, blue-blood names like Rockefeller, Hunt, Getty, Phipps and Du Pont.

In the late 1980s, the rich began to change. Soaring financial markets ushered in a new group of Wall Streeters, corporate raiders and tech pioneers. The number of billionaires jumped from 13 in 1982 to 67 in 1989. By 2000, with the bull market in full swing, the trickle turned into a tidal wave, and the population of millionaires more than tripled to eight million people—greater than the population of Sweden or Austria.

The rich became Richistanis—members of a distinct new generation of wealth.

Richistanis didn't inherit their wealth, but rose up through the ranks of the middle class or upper middle class to make it on their own. Paris Hilton aside, only 3 percent of today's multimillionaires are celebrities and less than 10 percent inherited their money.

They're also much younger than previous generations of rich people. "Before the 1990s, most of the wealthy I knew were retired, they were in their sixties or seventies," says Peter Scaturro, former CEO of U.S. Trust, the wealth management firm. "Now they're in their thirties and forties. They have a lot of runway left in front of them."

Richistan is also a country of deep divisions. The relatively homogenous culture of Old Money—with its boarding schools, social clubs, cultural institutions and sporty nicknames—has become atomized. Richistanis are far more diverse in terms of age, race, gender and geography. And they are more polarized politically, with a rising new generation of young, wealthy liberals squaring off against older-line Republicans.

The most surprising divide in Richistan, however, is between wealth levels. Just as the wealth disparities have grown between Richistan and the rest of the United States, they've also grown within Richistan, creating a new kind of upper-class warfare between the haves and have-mores.

Richistan, in fact, has at least three classes.

Lower Richistan

Lower Richistan is the sprawling suburbia of Richistan, with a population that's exploded to more than seven million households. Lower Richistanis live in McMansions, drive around in SUVs and relax in lawn furniture purchased from the Frontgate catalogue. Most of them are well-educated, work-a-day professionals: corporate executives, doctors, lawyers, bankers, designers, analysts and money

THE THREE LEVELS OF RICHISTAN

Lower Richistan

HOUSEHOLD NET WORTH: $1 million to $10 million

POPULATION: 7.5 million households

CHIEF SOURCE OF WEALTH: Salaries, small business, equity

AVERAGE 2006 SPENDING: Watches $2,100 * Cars $44,000 *
Jewelry $9,200 * Spa services $5,300

VALUE OF PRIMARY RESIDENCE: $810,000

Middle Richistan

HOUSEHOLD NET WORTH: $10 million to $100 million

POPULATION: More than 2 million households

CHIEF SOURCES OF WEALTH: Business ownership, equity, salaries

AVERAGE 2006 SPENDING: Watches $71,000 * Cars $158,000 *
Jewelry $126,000 * Spa services $42,000

VALUE OF PRIMARY RESIDENCE: $3.8 million

Upper Richistan

HOUSEHOLD NET WORTH: $100 million to $1 billion

POPULATION: In the thousands

CHIEF SOURCES OF WEALTH: Business ownership, equity

AVERAGE 2006 SPENDING: Watches $182,000 * Cars $311,000 *
Jewelry $397,000 * Spa services $169,000

VALUE OF PRIMARY RESIDENCE: $16.2 million

SOURCE: Federal Reserve Board, Elite Traveler/Prince & Associates

managers. More than half their wealth is derived from income, with another third coming from investment returns. In an increasingly global, high-tech, finance-oriented economy, Lower Richistanis have benefited from the growing demand for highly educated workers and rising pay at the top.

Lower Richistanis are conservative in their politics. A

majority of them voted for George W. Bush in the 2004 election, saying he was the best candidate to help improve their personal financial situation. They're also strong advocates of abolishing the estate tax, since most would be targets.

Yet behind their newfound success lies a nagging sense of insecurity. Lower Richistanis may have more money than 95 percent of Americans, but they're becoming poorer relative to their fellow Richistanis. The economic distance between the poorest Richistani and the richest has more than doubled over the past decade. The average income for the top 1 percent of income earners grew 57 percent between 1990 and 2004, yet it grew an even better 85 percent for the richest one-tenth of 1 percent.

When they go to cocktail parties or their kids' soccer games, Lower Richistanis run into crowds of people with vastly more wealth. So to keep up with their richer brethren, Lower Richistanis are spending more and borrowing heavily. In 2004, Richistan's inflation rate topped 6 percent—twice the broader inflation rate in the United States—driven by all those rich people vying for the same private schools, nannies, BMWs, Jimmy Choo shoes and beach homes. Lower Richistanis have taken on billions of dollars in debt over the past decade. About 20 percent of Lower Richistanis spent all of their income or more in 2004.

Many Richistanis say that Lower Richistanis don't even belong in their country. They refer to the Lowers as "affluent"—the ultimate Richistani insult. In the words of Andrew Carnegie, that great Richistani patriarch, Lower Richistanis represent "not wealth, but only competence."

So let's go a bit higher.

Mid∂le Richistan

In Middle Richistan, families have net worths of between $10 million and $100 million. Here too the population
has exploded, to more than 1.4 million. Yet life here is a little
more comfortable. The homes are bigger, the art is nicer and
most of the residents have vacation homes. Most Middle
Richistanis make their money from salaries, small businesses or investment returns. As you move from Lower to
Upper Richistan, however, the number of entrepreneurs and
business owners starts to increase. Middle Richistan has
twice as many entrepreneurs as Lower Richistan, showing
that the surest path to big wealth is starting your own
company and selling it.

Middle Richistanis are also more liberal than the Lowers. Most Middle Richistanis voted for John Kerry in the
last presidential election, even though they said Mr. Bush
would be better for their personal financial situation. The
Middle Richistanis placed a higher emphasis on education, environment, and technology policy.

Still, living in Middle Richistan has its price. The inflation
rate for Richistanis worth $30 million or more climbed
to more than 11 percent in 2004, almost three times the
national inflation rate. Since Middle Richistanis, as well
as their wealthier brethren, have grown richer at a faster
rate than Lower Richistanis, they have more to spend and
fewer worries about running out of money.

Upper Richistan

The penthouses of Upper Richistan are filled with families worth $100 million or more. Upper Richistan has a

population of thousands, though the exact numbers aren't known. Most made their money by starting their own companies and selling them, although CEOs and money managers (especially hedge funders) are rapidly joining the ranks.

The lives of Upper Richistanis have become incredibly complicated. To run them, they're creating "family offices"—large companies dedicated entirely to serving a family's day-to-day needs, from investments and legal work to travel plans and hiring house staff. Upper Richistanis rarely open their own mail or pay their own bills, which may help explain why the average annual spa bill in Upper Richistan is $107,000.

When you live in Upper Richistan, your entire philosophy of money changes. You realize that you can't possibly spend all of your fortune, or even part of it, in your lifetime and that your money will probably grow over the years even if you spend lavishly. So Upper Richistanis plan their finances for the next hundred years. They don't buy mutual funds; they buy timber land, oil rigs and office towers.

Still, Upper Richistanis have occasional feelings of inferiority. That's because they're being overshadowed by the residents of Billionaireville.

Billionaireville

Billionaireville had only 13 inhabitants in 1985. In 2006 there were more than 400, according to Forbes. Leslie Mandel, president of the New York–based Rich List Co., which tracks the wealthy, says her personal list has more than 1,000 billionaires in the United States, most of whom have stayed under the public radar.

The personal lives of billionaires are more like companies. Their homes are like hotels—sprawling campuses with their own logos, purchasing budgets and legions of staff. Ask a billionaire for his or her bank statement and you'll get a five-level flowchart of interlocking subsidiaries, holding companies, investment funds and foundations.

Billionaires have done especially well over the past decade. The total wealth held by the Forbes 400 has more than doubled since 1995, from $439 billion to more than $1 trillion today. Yet even billionaires are starting to feel common. Tim Blixseth, a billionaire timber baron and resort owner, told me about the time a multibillionaire came to his estate, which has its own private golf course. After playing 18 holes, the guest said he liked the place so much he wanted to buy it. He handed Tim a slip of paper with his offer: $400 million. Tim turned it down, but not without marveling at what could have become the ultimate impulse purchase.

"Now that guy," Blixseth said, "*he* was rich."

BEFORE we meet more Richistanis, let's take another look at how the world of the rich has changed—this time through the eyes of the people who serve them.

1

BUTLER BOOT CAMP

Housetraining the New Rich

Dawn Carmichael stands at attention, holding two plates of almond-crusted sea bass with Moroccan salsa. The blond, ex-Starbucks barista is dressed in a blue suit and white shirt, with a crisply folded napkin draped over her left arm. She's lined up with three other servers in the cavernous kitchen of the Starkey Mansion, a prim, Georgian home in downtown Denver. When they get the signal— two taps on the kitchen door—the group will march into the dining room, greet their 12 dinner guests and begin their first public performance of the Ballet of Service.

The Ballet of Service is a complex routine where all the waiters must serve the plates to guests in perfect sync. It takes hours of practice. And it is one of the most demanding skills taught here at the Starkey Mansion—better known as Butler Boot Camp.

Ms. Carmichael visualizes the routine: Serve to the left, take two steps to the right, shift the second plate from right hand to left, and serve again. When "addressing" the table, she must lean in far enough for a smooth plate delivery, but not so close as to make the guests uncomfortable. After serving, she's supposed to take one step back, wait for eye contact with the other servers and exit the room counterclockwise.

Each step must look like a choreographed dance, building to a climax called the "crossover"—a plate-juggling pas de deux in which the butlers slide the second plate from their right to left hand with a quick body pivot, creating the illusion that the plate is suspended in midair while it's being transferred.

The Ballet of Service is designed to show off all the desired traits of a butler-to-be—discipline, agility, poise and intimacy with tableware. And it's one of toughest training exercises here at Butler Boot Camp.

Four times a year, aspiring butlers from around the country converge for Boot Camp training at Starkey, officially known as the Starkey International Institute for Household Management. Their aim: to become masters at the care and feeding of the rich. For eight weeks, the students hole up inside the mansion to cook, clean, polish, dust, wash and fold. They learn how to iron a set of French cuffs in seconds flat. They're taught how to clip a 1926 Pardona cigar, how to dust a de Kooning canvas and how to pair an oaky chardonnay with roasted free-range game hen.

They learn how long it takes to clean a 45,000-square-foot mansion (20 to 30 hours depending on the art and antiques), where to find 1,020-thread-count sheets (Kreiss .com) and how to order Ben & Jerry's Chunky Monkey ice cream at midnight if your employer is on a yacht in the Mediterranean (a British concierge service). They will be able to divide a 30,000-square-foot home into "zones" for cleaning and maintenance. They will design "stationery wardrobes"—envelopes and letterhead specially designed to reflect the owner's wealth and social standing. They will be taught that sable stoles should never be stored in a cedar closet (it dries them out), and that Bentleys should never, ever be run through the car wash.

Most of the students live in the mansion during Boot Camp, following the strict Starkey rules. Everyone has to wear a uniform of khakis, crisp white shirts, blue blazers and brown shoes. First names are banned; everyone is "Mr." or "Ms." to stress the importance of boundaries. The students are required to rise from their seats every time a visitor enters the room. If there's a coffee cup that needs filling, a spoon that needs polishing or a visitor who needs welcoming, the Starkey students must spring into action. The butlers-to-be are so wired for service that when a class break is announced, they all pounce from their seats to fill each other's water glasses.

By the end of the course, the aspiring butlers will be masters at pampering the privileged. The rich, they will learn, like their shampoo bottles and toothpaste tubes always filled to the top. If their employers have four homes, chances are they'll want their dresser drawers and bathroom cabinets arranged exactly the same in every house, so they don't have to go searching for their socks or pills. And they learn that the rich live in constant fear of germs.

"They're health freaks," says Raymond Champion, Starkey's chief instructor, standing at the whiteboard in Starkey's basement classroom. "These people are very successful and guess what, they want to live forever. These are very germ-oriented people. Get used to it. Germs are *huge* in this world."

No butler leaves Starkey without learning about the two other priorities for the wealthy—pets and collections. At Starkey these are known as "BYJ" categories, as in Bet Your Job.

During one class, Champion tells a story of a Southern family that had an entire mansion filled with birdcalls, which the butler had to dust and maintain every day. There was the guy with 500 cars that needed hand-washing and the rich heiress who had a barn full of cats and employed three full-time litter changers and a full-time bird feeder to pour seeds around the barn to attract birds to entertain the cats.

"The guy who fed the birds got paid more than any of us," he says.

Most of all, the Starkey students learn never to judge their employers, whom they call "principals." If a principal wants to feed her shih tzu braised beef tenderloin steaks every night, the butler should serve it up with a smile. If a principal is in Palm Beach and wants to send his jet to New York to pick up a Chateau LaTour from his South Hampton cellar, the butler makes it happen, no questions asked.

Starkey students pay more than $12,000 for Boot Camp. While that may sound steep, the payoff is even bigger. Butlering has become one of the fastest-growing jobs in the United States. With so many Richistanis needing so many butlers, demand and pay are soaring. A good Starkey graduate can start at $80,000 to $120,000 a year— not to mention free room and board at the mansion.

First, they have to get through the Ballet. Tonight, Dawn Carmichael and the butlers are nervous. It's their first Ballet and they haven't had much practice. Dawn gets her signal and leads the other three servers into the dining room. Under a crystal chandelier, the dinner guests are arrayed at the table with perfectly spaced sets of flatware, finger bowls and assorted glasses.

The first plates go down smoothly. But on the crossover, Dawn moves before the other three servers. She freezes, trying to get back in sync. The other three also freeze. The guests glance up at the four panicked butlers standing motionless with their plates of sea bass.

Finally, the butlers nod, serve the plates and quickly march out of the room.

"I lost the rhythm," Dawn says to the other butlers in the kitchen. "Oh man, was that bad."

James Hopkins, a fresh-faced college grad from Maine, is equally disappointed. "It felt awkward," he said. "We looked like robots."

The next morning, Raymond Champion takes the class to task. A former marine, whose specialties include martial arts, weapons training and decorative baking, Champion has little patience for sloppiness. He served as an enlisted aide to several generals and served in combat during the first Gulf War. With his six-foot-two frame, square jaw and impeccable manners, Champion makes for the perfect drill sergeant for Butler Boot Camp.

"I was disappointed," he tells the students the next morning, standing in front of his whiteboard. "Very disappointed."

Champion says that aside from the crossover, there were other foul-ups. He looks at John Leech, a flamboyant bed-and-breakfast owner from upstate New York. Leech was in charge of wine during the dinner and his job was to keep all the glasses exactly half full. Yet he allowed some glasses to drop to a quarter full before refilling. Champion also says Leech paid too much attention to the guests' conversation, rather than maintaining the detached attentiveness required of a butler.

"What can I say, I'm a very social person," Leech tells me later. "The guests were all telling interesting stories so it was hard not to listen. And I didn't keep the glasses full because I felt like I was being compulsive. But Champion was right."

The next night the class hosts another formal dinner. It goes perfectly. Dawn leads an expertly choreographed Ballet of Service. Leech keeps the wineglasses exactly half full. And he successfully ignores the guests' stories.

Champion greets them the next morning with a broad smile.

"Congratulations," he says. "Now *that* was service."

Jeeves 2.0

The story of the butler boom is the story of all that has changed about American wealth over the past 15 years. It's not just a tale of more rich people needing more butlers, though that's a big part of it. It's also the story of a new culture of wealth emerging in America, driven by a new kind of rich person.

For much of the 20th century, butlers were a dying breed. The grand old mansions built during the Gilded Age and Roaring Twenties, with their armies of footmen, cooks, maids, drivers and butlers, began to fall into disrepair in the 1960s and 1970s as wealth creation slowed. The demand for butlers faded, along with many of the Old Money fortunes. Culturally, the rich fell out of favor, along with the notion of household staff. Butlers became relics of a distant world, existing only in P. G. Wodehouse novels and period films like *Remains of the Day.*

"The whole concept of a high level of service in the household vanished," says Mary Starkey, Starkey International's founder. "It wasn't fashionable to have help."

Now, butlers are making a comeback. The vast new population of Richistanis, with their huge homes, multitude of toys and large lifestyles, has created new demand for household help. Maids, nannies, personal assistants and private security guards are proliferating. Catering to the rich—once considered dead-end service work—is now a hot career track. And of all the occupations, the butler has seen the most dramatic transformation in skills and pay.

Butler placement agencies in New York, Florida, Texas and California have hundreds of postings for jobs and not enough qualified applicants to fill them. Butlers looking for work today often have a choice of working in a penthouse in Manhattan, a beach compound in St. Bart's or a log mansion in Aspen. A new Internet site for household managers, called EstateJobs.com, had more than 100 postings only three months after its launch in 2005. The ads, with their "Come-to-the-Beautiful-Bahamas" sales pitches, sound more like travel promotions than job classifieds. Here are two ads from late 2006:

> Live in beautiful Palm Beach for 6 months and Boston and the Cape for the other 6 months. Live-in position as a butler/valet. Taking care of Mister's wardrobe, inventory, light cooking for lunches when the chef is off, entertaining and guest care.
>
> Living quarters are a professionally decorated 1 bedroom house on property in Florida and studio apartments in Boston and the Cape.

Or, for those who prefer the Hamptons:

> This New York City family needs someone extremely organized. They summer in the Hamptons and need someone to assist in running and staffing their new summer home—now under construction—with housekeepers, chefs and whatever else is deemed necessary. They also need someone techie—Mac and BlackBerry savvy to set up systems in the new beach house and facilitate entertaining, travel arrangements and coordinate with all appropriate vendors. Other duties involve shopping for presents.

The Bureau of Labor Statistics doesn't keep stats on butlers (they're working on it). Yet agencies say the number of rich clients looking to hire household managers and butlers has been rising every year since the late 1990s.

"It's not a very publicized career track," says David Gonzalez, president and founder of the Domestic Placement Network in California, which also owns EstateJobs .com. "But there's incredible demand. The number of wealthy people and the size of their homes are exploding. Suddenly they're realizing they need help."

One of Gonzalez's clients, for instance, is buying 15 homes for various family members and needs a staff of about 40 to 50 to run them all. Keith Greenhouse, of the Pavillion Agency in New York, says he "can't possibly fill every job order we get." While "finding good help" has always been the curse of the wealthy, it's even harder today with the sudden increase in Richistanis.

That's fueled a surge in butler training. The Professional Services and Domestic Institute in Ohio, another butler academy, is planning to open schools around the country to meet rising demand. Carol Scudere, Professional's founder, says all 40 of the butlers from her last five classes got jobs before or shortly after graduation. Most started at $75,000 or more. The acronym CHM, for Certified Household Manager, can now be found on business cards alongside more traditional designations like CFA and JD.

"My biggest problem now is finding students," Scudere says. "There are plenty of jobs for them."

Starkey, however, has become the headquarters of the butler boom, and it is the oldest and largest butler school in the country. Mary Louise Starkey, a chipper dynamo of a woman, wears bright lipstick, dramatic scarves and a permanent smile. Her business card reads: "Mary Starkey— First Lady of Service."

Starkey grew up in a moneyed family and learned firsthand about the secrets to hiring good help. Her family owned a Coca-Cola bottler in South Dakota, and her father's family had come from a rich clan in southern Illinois.

"I used to go to visit my dad's family home and this

fellow Walter was the chauffeur," she says. "This was my introduction to the service world. The relationships were formed after so many years, and Walter would do anything for my grandfather. He was proud that his role was in service."

Her family expected her to go to college, find a husband and settle down with a family. Yet Starkey had other plans. After attending a Catholic university in Denver for a few years, she quit and put herself through Metropolitan State College and got a degree in community services development. After working a series of jobs at various charities and foundations, she quit and went looking for other work.

One day, an acquaintance called looking for someone to clean his house. Starkey needed the money, since she had just divorced and was struggling to raise two sons. She took the job and, spotting a potential business opportunity, started a cleaning service. Within weeks she was flooded with calls and work. She later started a placement company for maids and nannies. One day a Middle Eastern prince who was studying in Denver called wanting a butler. She looked around town for butler agencies and couldn't find one. So she decided to start her own.

Starkey quickly realized, however, that the rich were changing. The Old Money families with their white-gloved, balding butlers were gone. In their place was a new generation of young, self-made entrepreneurs and finance types who worked round the clock and built tech-loaded mansions. These New Rich didn't want a stuffy house mascot. They needed a guy (or, more often, a woman) who could get things done and manage their increasingly complicated homes.

The perfect butler would be able to oversee 30 vendors—from the pool cleaners and landscapers to the home-theater installer and dog groomer. She would be able to manage a house budget of $2 million a year and detail every item on an Excel spreadsheet. She would be a computer geek who could program the lights on the smart-home system, network the computers at the Montana ranch and reset the home-alarm system from a laptop miles away. She would be a travel agent who could book the next flight to Paris and get a prime room at the George V. And she would be a leader who could oversee a team of grumpy maids, crazy chefs, erudite nannies and surly security guards.

Richistanis didn't want butlers. They wanted a chief operating officer for My Life Inc. So in 1990, Mary Starkey sat down with a dictionary and started looking for a word to describe the new style of butler.

Eventually she came up with her own term: "household manager." With the new title, Mary Starkey rebranded the butler and launched an industry. She founded the Starkey International Institute for Household Management, starting in an old house in downtown Denver and later moving to the Starkey Mansion, a red-brick Georgian mansion just behind the state capitol.

Starkey taught the first classes herself, then gradually hired staff, including Mr. Champion and William Altoff, the culinary instructor, who has served as the valet and cook to three U.S. presidents and managed the vice president's home for Al Gore. Other teachers pop in and out, including a security expert, human resource exec, limousine expert, jeweler, linens specialist, smart-home system retailer and sommelier.

Starkey now runs nine classes a year, educating about 100 budding butlers in 2006. It holds four annual Boot Camps along with an abridged four-week "certified manager's program," and a four-day software course.

Starkey's revenues are growing at more than 30 percent a year, totaling $2 million in 2005. Most of Ms. Starkey's sales come from spin-off businesses. She sells her own software, a household manager textbook (650 pages) and an "owner's manual" for principals who have never hired household staff.

Once a year, Starkey hosts a conference called "Restoring the Art," where the growing army of household managers from around the country get together to swap stories and tips. She's also writing a new book on etiquette and launching a program to educate family offices. The biggest profits come from placement and consulting, since she gets a 25 to 35 percent commission on the first year's salary for each hire.

With all the household managers she's graduating, Ms. Starkey still doesn't have enough students to meet demand. On the third floor of the Starkey Mansion, a team of placement workers receives dozens of calls a day from newly rich homeowners looking for help. A large chalkboard on the wall lists more than a dozen requests for household managers.

> Certified Household Manager needed for large home—
> $90,000 a year.
> Certified Household Manager—qualified for entertainment,
>   large construction projects, jets, boats, administration.

By placing so many butlers, Ms. Starkey has gained an innate understanding of the new Richistanis. Often, she has to focus more on what they say than on what they do. The newly wealthy, for instance, love to say that they're simple middle-class people, even if they happen to own four homes and a Gulfstream. On the first day of Butler Boot Camp, Ms. Starkey tells her class the story of a Connecticut hedge-fund manager who sought her advice on hiring a butler.

"I got there, and this couple said, 'We're really simple, casual people. We just need someone to do a little cooking and cleaning.' Well, the wife is this stunning former dancer and she's wearing all Chanel and Burberry. They have Masters' art all over the walls, they have a lap pool in the basement with palm trees and a 5,000-bottle wine cellar. When I ask to see the table settings, the wife shows me her 20-piece Christofle flatware, with the fish knives and the whole shebang. Nothing was casual or simple about their life. 'Just a little cooking and cleaning.' Wanna bet?"

Ms. Starkey also has to work around the tendency of today's rich to get chummy with their help. Her clients have perfected the art of faux populism and hate the idea of being stuffy bosses. They want to show they can be "friends" with their help—even when they're not. To draw the line, Ms. Starkey bans the use of first names in the mansion, insisting that everyone be called "Mr." or "Ms." She makes the same request of employers.

"If your employer says to you, 'Oh just call me Chandra and this is Jim,' do not accept," Starkey tells the class. "Have you ever asked for a raise from 'Chandra'? You're not best buds. People project all kinds of relationships on to you . . . mother, daughter, father, sister, friend. But you are a professional. Boundaries are critical."

To cater to this new breed of rich person, Ms. Starkey

had to create a whole new kind of butler program, far removed from the Old World butler academies in Britain. Sure, her butlers learn to cook and clean. But they also learn to become executives of the sprawling, modern, six-star resorts Richistanis call home.

So Butler Boot Camp is built around an intricate management system called the Service Management Model. Butlers spend more than 100 hours learning the system, which they're expected to use wherever they go. It's a kind of butler's business plan, used to reassure today's management-obsessed, flowchart-friendly wealthy that they're making a good hire.

The model starts with the Service Vision, akin to a corporate strategy statement, where the butler details exactly what kind of atmosphere he or she is trying to create in the house (formal, informal; beach party pad or Old World estate). That's followed by the People Section, in which the butler details the family tree, family goals, values, lifestyle and schedules. The Environment Section describes the physical dimensions of the house and grounds.

The core of the system is the Standards Matrix, which includes the "10 Service Standards and Perpetual Service Variables." It gives "baseline" standards for certain levels of service. For instance, should you wash the dog bed once or twice a day? Do employers like their T-shirts hung instead of folded? Do they prefer "plated" or family-style service at dinner? Household managers even work up a "flavor profile" for all family members, determining, for instance, if one's comfort foods are meatloaf and potatoes or butter-poached lobster with champagne gelée.

As the job of butlering has changed so has the profile of

the butlers. Gone are the stiff, jowly old men who were born into the trade. Today's household managers are younger, often college-educated, and more likely to be women. Of the 10 students enrolled in the Starkey class I visited, half were women. Most were in their 30s and 40s and most had come from some kind of service profession, like hotels, resorts or restaurants. All claimed to be committed to something called "the service heart."

If you ask any butlers-in-training why they decided to spend the rest of their lives catering to the whims of the rich, they'll inevitably mention their "service heart." Dawn Carmichael says that she discovered her service heart when she worked briefly as a household assistant for a wealthy ranch owner. She helped maintain his two homes, prepared his food, helped him entertain guests and planned his trips.

"I loved knowing what made him happy," she says. "I sectioned his grapefruit every morning just the way he liked it and I always kept the TV tuned to channel 36, which was his favorite. I would sometimes ask myself, 'Why is it so important to me to get him the right kind of potato chips? Am I sick? What is wrong with me?' But then I came to Starkey and realized that there are others out there like me. I really feel like I've found out what I was meant to do."

James Hopkins, the 22-year-old college grad with a degree in hospitality, discovered his service heart growing up near Bar Harbor, Maine. His father was a fisherman and the family didn't have much money. James started mowing lawns in the summer and landed a job at one of the sprawling oceanside estates in nearby Seal Harbor, cutting the grass and maintaining the grounds. The family took a liking to him, and he started doing other small chores—gardening, landscaping, docking their boat—and even some work in the house.

"I realized I liked being around wealth," he says. "You know, the family is flown to France for lunch, or they decide to have drinks on the yacht. If I can play a part in making that happen, I'd be pretty happy."

So Mr. Hopkins borrowed $20,000 in student loans to get a college degree in hospitality. Then he borrowed another $12,000 to attend Starkey.

"I'm kind of nervous," Hopkins said on the first day of class. "I'm kind of young for this kind of work. But I'm ready to learn."

Kevin Stafford discovered his service heart behind a bar. Stafford, a 48-year-old Floridian with a bushy red mustache, thick glasses and earnest demeanor, worked for years as bartender at Bernard's Surf, a lounge in Cocoa Beach, Florida. Bernard's was a big hangout for NASA engineers, and Stafford spent his days and nights serving up cold beers and gossiping about the space program.

"I spent a lot of time talking about O-rings and fuel gels," Stafford told me.

One night several years ago, a young couple came in from out of town. They ordered a vodka screwdriver and a Stoli martini straight up. Stafford chatted with them and learned they were in town for vacation. A year later, the couple came back and Stafford asked, "Screwdriver and Stoli martini?"

"They were amazed that I remembered," he says. After chatting with Stafford some more, the man turned to his wife and said, "This is where I'm going to make my fortune, and when I do, I'm going to hire Kevin here to be our butler."

Sure enough, the couple moved to Florida and made a fortune from Orlando real estate. They've just put the finishing touches on an 11,000-square-foot penthouse in Cocoa Beach and hired Stafford to manage it. They also hired Stafford's wife, bought him a new truck and agreed to renovate his house. On top of that, they agreed to pay for his training at Starkey.

"I'm so grateful," Stafford says after class one day, tears welling up in his eyes. "It's like a dream."

BUTLER Boot Camp, however, turned out to be less enchanting for Mr. Stafford and many of his classmates. Midway through Starkey's 79th Boot Camp, the stress started to show. The night before the formal dinner, a dispute erupted over a felt table pad. The pad was too small, and Dawn and another student—a Bermudan named Beverly—got into a brief argument over how to fix it. Beverly said it was her job and she'd handle it, and Dawn erupted, saying, "Don't *even* talk to me like that." Champion overheard the spat and hauled Dawn into the study for a private chat.

"He said, 'What if the principal had been there?'" Dawn recalls. "He said my opinion doesn't matter unless it's asked for. And he said if he heard me speak to anyone like that again, I'd be out of Starkey."

Dawn burst out of the room crying and walked outside into a blizzard. She sat in her car in the parking lot for over an hour, trying to decide whether to stay at Starkey or drive away.

"I realized that I belonged there," she said. "And I realized that I came to Starkey to learn about grace and deportment, and that's what Champion was teaching me."

She brushed herself off, went back in and completed the course.

James Hopkins also had his low moments. Though poised for a 22-year-old, he still had college-age tics that reflected poorly on a future butler. He said "yeah" instead of "yes." He chewed on his fingernails. He rarely looked you straight in the eye when speaking.

Champion pounded him daily, correcting his "yeahs" and pointing out the nail-biting.

"He kept on me," Hopkins said. "But I needed it."

One day, Champion spent over two hours teaching the students how to open the front door for guests—a must for any butler. The butler, he explained, should draw the door open quickly and smoothly, but not so fast as to be startling. He or she should take one step back while the door opens, keeping the shoulders exactly parallel with the door.

"Everything we do should be like a production," he says. "In this case, it's like opening the curtain onto the stage of the house."

At one point Kevin Stafford had to ask for help from two other classmates because he was falling behind on his workbook.

"There was one point where we weren't sure whether Stafford was going to graduate," John Leech says. "He pulled through."

Some of the students say privately that Champion pushed too hard, that he got upset over small details.

When I mention it, Champion tells the story of how he served in the first Gulf War and lost a buddy during a desert raid. Going into battle, Champion told his friend that they would fight and come back together. His friend never made it back.

"It's the same with these students," he says. "I will never give up on them, I will never let them down."

By graduation day the butlers are all smiles. Stafford is headed back to Florida to work at the penthouse. Two other Boot Campers got hired to manage a sprawling estate in Washington, with one of them starting at $120,000 a year. Leech was offered a job at a plush new luxury resort in Vanuatu, where a one-week stay costs couples $250,000 (he turned it down). And Hopkins got a job in Florida working for a money manager. Ms. Carmichael had a few offers, though she hadn't landed a job yet.

"I love this work," she says, walking down the front steps of the Starkey Mansion after the graduation ceremony. "I know that this is what I was put on this earth to do."

Housetraining the New Rich

Just as new butlers need training, so do the New Rich. Since most of today's Richistanis grew up middle class, they're not used to having servants. They're used to doing things themselves, and they're uncomfortable with the stuffy formalities that often come with hiring house staff.

Take the case of Bob, a real-estate tycoon and ranch

owner in the Far West. Bob, his wife and two kids live on 800 acres of land with 10,000 square feet of living space. They have a main house, art studio, hunting cabin and other buildings scattered around the property. To manage it all, Bob hired six house staff, including a household manager from Starkey.

Getting used to living with all those strangers took time. Especially since he grew up in what he calls a "Wonder Years" environment, in postwar, middle-class suburbia.

"It's bizarre," he says. "It's not as glamorous as it sounds to have a house staff. You have all these people touching everything from your underwear to your medicine. It's not really our preference."

The reason he hired all that help was to give him and his wife more time with their kids. Since they run their own business, they're not home much and wanted to spend their free time with their two sons, rather than cooking, cleaning or mowing the lawn.

"When we're home, we wanted to do nothing but spend time with our boys. We don't do any household chores, we don't fix anything, we don't clean anything. Our goal was to spend 55 hours a week with our kids, which we have now achieved."

Yet Bob quickly discovered that managing a house staff has its own headaches.

"Suddenly there's all this funky politics going on in your house. Like the housekeeper might be nice to us, but she's threatening to the other employees. So we had to get rid of that housekeeper."

His first household manager was even worse. An exacting woman who specialized in formal entertainment, she aspired to work in a house that threw lavish parties for prominent guests. Instead, she got Bob and his family, whose idea of a good time is a mountain-bike ride around the ranch followed by a big salad. Most nights after dinner, they read to the kids or watch 1940s comedies on DVD. Bob rarely wears a suit, drives a six-year-old car and rarely throws parties.

The household manager was deeply disappointed.

"We weren't the rich, famous people she was hoping for," Bob says.

She tried to convert them, anyway. Every Friday night, she presented a formal dinner for the family. Bob, his wife and two sons would sit down at the dinner table and the household manager would serve them from silver platters. She even bought an expensive steam press to smooth the napkins into perfect triangles.

"During one of these dinners my wife and I turned to each other and said, 'What's the deal? Does she think this is how we're supposed to live?'"

One time, Bob's wife insisted that the household manager call her by her first name. Her response, "Yes, Mrs. . . ."

Eventually, Bob got fed up and hired a new household manager, this one from Starkey. So far, he's worked out perfectly. A former bank worker, the household manager runs the house the way Bob likes it—like a business. And Bob pays him accordingly, at $80,000 a year.

"What Starkey does is teach a business degree," Bob says. "With my household manager, we have everything on Excel spreadsheets. I get summary reports on the weekend and e-mails throughout the day. All the credit cards and checks run on Quicken and we run our home like a business, with a consolidated P&L and everything."

He also likes the fact that his household manager seems to enjoy service.

"We've had plenty of surly people work for us, and you can tell, they resent it. Our crew now, they understand that we're just normal people and that we have them there so we can spend time with our kids. I think they respect that."

Yet Bob still has moments when he wonders how his life got so complicated. Aside from his six staff—the household manager, cleaning woman, assistant, landscaper and her two laborers—he estimates that he has about 200 vendors who regularly come to the house.

"I just learned that we have a potassium expert because we grow grapes," he says. "I never thought I'd have a soil doctor. And we have this woman who comes in to do faux French finishes on our cabinets. And a special guy who comes in to fix our French faucets. It turns out you can't just call A1 plumbing to fix an Etoile faucet.

"I get e-mails during the day saying 'Please approve $8,000 payment for aerator for the north pond.' Our grocery list is done on an Excel spreadsheet. We even have another Excel spreadsheet for our pool temperatures. That's pretty strange."

He sums up his new life with a story about a mouse.

"The other day we saw a mouse in the house. Before, I would have just gotten a broom and gotten rid of the thing. But now it's different. I e-mailed the household manager. He called the vendor, a pest-control firm, and the pest-control firm caught the mouse. Then the household manager directed two other staff members to dispose of the mouse. That's five people to catch a mouse, instead of a broom. It all seemed normal at the time. But then I thought about it, and I wondered, how did our lives get like this?"

How did Richistanis get where they are? And how did so many get so wealthy? Despite all the headlines about CEO pay and "winner-take-all" salaries, most of today's multi-millionaires and billionaires owe their fortunes to a different, and broader, series of economic changes.

2

THE THIRD WAVE

The Era of the Instapreneur

The latest American wealth boom is at once unprece-
dented and conventional. While its size and scale have
never been matched in history, its root causes are similar to
those that sparked the country's two other big booms, the
Gilded Age and the Roaring Twenties.

In his book *Wealth and Democracy*, Kevin Phillips
writes that large spikes in American wealth have been
driven by the same convergence of forces: new technologies, a rise in financial speculation and governments supportive of free markets and the wealthy. Citing the work of
Austrian economist Joseph Schumpeter, Phillips argues
that new technologies and speculative financial markets

have historically fed off each other to create record numbers of millionaires and billionaires.

"In an age of excess, technology and finance joined to lead the way," he writes.

The first of the nation's major wealth waves was the Gilded Age, which began after the Civil War. Railroads, oil and steel were the new technologies of the day, while the emergence of a national banking system and the rise of stocks provided the financial fuel. Government encouraged the big oil, sugar, whisky and sugar trusts, and the U.S. Senate was packed with free-marketeering millionaires. The number of millionaires in the United States soared to about 4,500 by 1900. The biggest American fortunes rose from $10 million or $20 million in the mid-1800s to between $200 million and $300 million at the turn of the century. Standard Oil founder John D. Rockefeller exploded all records when he became a billionaire in the early 1900s. Wealth became highly concentrated geographically, with most of the fortunes residing in the Northeast. It also became concentrated economically. By 1890, as much as half of the country's wealth was held by the richest 1 percent of families.

The Gilded Age was followed by the second wave, the Roaring Twenties. Wartime profits and the advent of radio, moving pictures, autos and telephones created a surge in consumer demand. Lower taxes on dividends, a rise in the stock market and an increase in mergers combined to produce a new generation of finance-driven fortunes. The number of millionaires in the United States jumped from between 5,000 and 7,000 in 1921 to between 25,000 and 35,000 at the market's peak in 1929. In 1929, just before the market crash, the nation's wealthiest 1 percent still held nearly half the nation's wealth.

The postwar period, from the mid-1940s to the 1960s, also produced significant wealth. The Dow Jones Industrial Average, after two years in the doldrums, began to march higher. The victory over Japan and Germany opened up new global markets for companies that had thrived during the war. And American consumers went on a national shopping spree for cars, homes and appliances. Yet unlike the previous booms, the economic gains in the 1950s and 1960s were spread more broadly throughout the population. The rich actually *lost* ground during the postwar decades. The share of the nation's wealth held by the top 1 percent fell dramatically, from about 48 percent of the total, to just over 20 percent in the mid to late 1970s, leading economists Claudia Goldin and Robert Margo to label the period as the Great Compression. Culturally and politically, the rich fell out of favor:

> The middle class ethos ruled . . . the rich had become 'inconspicuous consumers,' either suffering from a guilt complex or afraid of giving visible offense. Their big houses had been sold off to become orphanages or old-age homes and fewer upper-income families had servants.

In the 1980s, the trend started reversing. With the rise of information technologies, capital markets and deregulation in government, the wealthy started to regain economic ground. The share of wealth held by the top 1 percent jumped to 30 percent in 1989, and has since risen to 33 percent.

While the 1980s came to be known as the "decade of greed" (following Gordon Gekko's line from the film *Wall Street* that "Greed is right. Greed works"), the decade turned out to be a mild prelude to the 1990s and early 2000s. The current wealth boom—let's call it the Third Wave—shares many of the same characteristics as the Gilded Age and the Roaring Twenties, with its convergence of technology, finance and free-market policies.

Yet the Third Wave has far surpassed the previous two waves. Half of America's total wealth has been created over the past 10 years. Rockefeller's $1 billion would be worth $14 billion today—less than the net worth of *each* of the five offspring of Wal-Mart founder Sam Walton.

The Third Wave also stands out globally. For the first time ever, the United States in 2004 surpassed Europe in the population of millionaires. In 2005, the United States cranked out 227,000 new financial millionaires (those with investible assets of more than $1 million). China, despite all the talk about its new wealth, added only 20,000 new financial millionaires in 2005, and its total millionaire population is one-hundredth of America's. India has only 83,000 millionaires—about the same as North Carolina.

The current wealth boom is the result of this classic convergence of economic forces—the rise of financial markets, new technologies and a freer flow of goods and information around the world. Yet it is the growth in finance, more than any other factor, that is driving the Third Wave and allowing people to become richer, faster than ever before.

More Money = More Wealth

The two words that private bankers like to hear most are "liquidity event." A liquidity event is the magic moment when an entrepreneur or corporate executive sells his or her stake in a company for truckloads of cash. Bankers love liquidity events, since they give them an instant pile of money to manage. So do the entrepreneurs and executives. In the Third Wave, liquidity events have become the most common source of real riches, outpacing inheritance, income and other sources.

Behind all these liquidity events is a broader shift in the world of finance. Years of low interest rates around the world, along with growing retirement accounts, rising corporate profits and increased global savings (China alone holds more than $1.7 trillion in savings deposits), have created a huge new wave of money. Global pension, insurance and mutual funds have $46 trillion at their disposal, up almost a third from 2000. In the same period, global central-bank reserves have doubled to $4 trillion, and other gauges of available capital have risen as well. While Americans may not be saving much, families abroad are saving much greater shares of their incomes.

All this cash piling up around the world has created what Fed Chairman Ben Bernanke once labeled the "global savings glut." Others have called it the "Wall of Money."

In reality, it's more like a river of money, coursing around the world, carving out new economic tributaries and looking for outlets. Stocks have been the most visible outlets. Since 1990 the value of all stocks traded in the United

States skyrocketed from $3 trillion in 1990 to more than $17 trillion today. Even after the stock slump of the early 2000s, market indexes continued to march higher, with the Dow breaking new records in 2007.

The river of money has also flooded into so-called alternative investments, like hedge funds, private-equity funds and venture capital. There are now more than 3,000 hedge funds managing more than $1 trillion. Private-equity firms and venture capitalists have more than $500 billion at their disposal. There's so much money pouring into hedge funds and venture-capital firms that they're actually turning away investors. (As we'll see in a later chapter, getting rejected by hedge funds and private-equity firms has created new miseries for rich investors.)

From stock markets and alternative investments, the surge of cash is also finding its way to individuals. Most Richistanis got where they are by tapping into this global river of cash—usually by starting their own companies. Others got there by being executives and dipping into the river through stock-based pay.

Today's Richistanis generally fall into one of five categories:

1. **Founders.** These are the entrepreneurs who started their own companies and sold their shares to investors through an initial public offering. Most of the Forbes list falls into this category, from Bill Gates and Sheldon Adelson to Larry Ellison and Michael Dell. More than 4,000 private companies have sold stock to the public through IPOs since 1995, raising $500 billion in cash.

2. **Stakeholders.** These are executives (nonfounders) who have stakes in a private company, then cash out when it goes public. When delivery giant UPS went public in 1999, dozens of top executives and managers who started out as drivers and package sorters became millionaires. There are now hundreds of "Microsoft millionaires"—Microsoft employees who worked at the company from its beginning and have made millions on their company stock. Google has created countless paper millionaires following its IPO and set off a mini-real-estate boom in the tony California community of Atherton. As one house buyer told *The Wall Street Journal,* "I started aggressively looking because I didn't want to get caught in the Google wave." When Austin-based CyBer-Corp was acquired by Charles Schwab in 2000, more than 100 staffers—including administrative assistants—became millionaires.

3. **The Acquired.** These are entrepreneurs or executives who sell their firms to another company or buyer for stock or cash. Driven by increased global competition and consolidation, companies have made more than 108,000 acquisitions since 1995, totaling $11 trillion.

4. **Money Movers.** These are the people who direct and invest this river of cash and keep a share for themselves. Wall Street banks paid out more than $36 billion in bonuses for 2006, with Goldman Sachs alone doling out $16 billion to its employees. Hedge-fund managers now make investment bankers look middle class (or Middle Richistani) by comparison, with the top three fund managers earning

more than $1 billion in 2004. The 25 highest-paid fund managers each made more than $130 million in 2004.

5. **Salaried Rich.** The pay of U.S. CEOs has ballooned to more than 170 times the average worker's pay, up from 40 times in the 1970s. Most of that jump in pay is tied to stock. Former ExxonMobil chief Lee Raymond received a $69.7 million compensation package and a $98 million pension payout in 2005, based on earnings results that analysts said were driven more by oil prices than by Mr. Raymond's keen management skills. Executives in Silicon Valley's 150 biggest tech companies exercised more than $1.84 billion in stock options in fiscal 2005, up 77 percent from 2003, according to compensation-research firm Equilar. Hank McKinnell, Pfizer Inc.'s former chairman and CEO, received a pay package potentially worth $200 million after he took early retirement.

Executives of well-established companies can now amass the kind of wealth once reserved for risk-taking entrepreneurs. UnitedHealth Group awarded almost $2 billion in stock options and compensation to chairman and CEO William McGuire over the past 15 years, although he later came under investigation by the Securities and Exchange Commission for stock-option policies. Bear Stearns Cos.' chairman and chief executive officer James Cayne holds a company stake, including stock and options, that reached a value of $1.02 billion in 2006, while Forbes recently named Lehman Bros. chief Dick Fuld as a billionaire.

Managers two or three levels down the corporate ladder are also racking up millions in pay. There were more than 4,700 corporate managers who were paid more than

$2 million last year in total compensation or stock options. In the San Francisco area alone, 641 executives earned more than $1 million in 2005.

According to a survey by Prince & Associates, more than 60 percent of individuals worth $10 million or more reported their source of wealth as "equity" or "post-equity"—meaning that stock was their main, initial source of wealth.

"That tells me that a lot of these people started their own business in some way," says Russ Alan Prince, Prince's founder.

Or they simply run them. About 23 percent of those worth $10 million or more reported their source of wealth as "executive," his survey showed. Inherited wealth accounted for only 10 percent of the total, while celebrities accounted for a minuscule 3 percent (what they lack in numbers they make up for in publicity).

Of course, the sources of wealth change as you move up the wealth ladder. The ranks of salaried rich and non-founder executives start to thin as you get to $25 million and above—a stratum dominated by entrepreneurs. Inherited wealth also starts to become more scarce as you get above $25 million.

Instapreneurs

Aside from changing the size and number of today's fortunes, the river of money has also changed the fundamental *way* people become rich today. For most of the 20th century, getting rich was incremental. If you worked for a company, you scrimped and saved your way to modest wealth. If you started a business, you grew it store by store, truck by truck, loan by loan. Most business owners had to plow their profits back into the business to keep expanding. It usually took a lifetime, if not generations, to build a business of any size. And there were few opportunities to cash out, since mergers and IPOs were rare.

In Richistan, wealth is sudden. The river of money has supercharged the process of getting rich. The salaried wealthy can now earn huge salaries, with built-in liquidity events, golden parachutes and other stock-related bonuses. For entrepreneurs, the river of money has accelerated the time it takes to start, grow and sell a company. Venture-capital firms have allowed entrepreneurs to instantly raise millions for their start-ups. Stock markets, hedge funds, private-equity firms and mergers have created new opportunities to cash out.

All that cash, combined with new technologies and globalization, has shortened the time it takes to launch a company and sell it for a liquidity event. It has also increased the value of assets, since there is now so much cash looking for investments. As a result, the entrepreneur has given way to the Instapreneur. An Instapreneur can launch a company with venture capital, expand to a global market and cash out through an IPO or sale—all within a few years or even months. For Instapreneurs, the primary goal isn't to build a business for generations. The goal is the "exit strategy" and the largest, fastest windfall possible.

Today's Instapreneurs can launch multiple companies over their lifetimes. Jared Polis, a technology whiz from Boulder, has founded more than a dozen companies (most tech-related) and made more than $600 million by selling them to competitors—all by the age of 31. Electronic-information wizard Jeff Parker launched three market-data companies that he sold to Thomson Financial in the mid-1980s. Then he went on to launch a fourth—CCBN—that he also sold to Thomson in 2004.

"Technology, access to capital and liquidity opportunities have all created faster cycle times when it comes to starting your own business," says Parker. "Once you start a business, and you're in the fray, you oftentimes spot another business opportunity and you can do it again."

The rewards for selling out have also gotten larger. With so much money searching for investment returns, the prices of valuable assets have soared. Iranian immigrants Paul Merage and his brother David launched Hot Pockets—the foil-wrapped frozen snacks—in the early 1990s and sold the business to Nestlé in 2002 for $2.6 billion. Haim Saban, a media magnate, merged his cartoon channel with Fox in 1995, then pocketed more than $1.7 billion when he sold it to Disney in 2001. Liquor magnate Sidney Frank created a new brand of vodka, called Grey Goose, and sold it to Bacardi for $2.3 billion.

Other Factors

Of course, the river of money and Instapreneurs aren't the only reasons we have so many new rich people. Government policy has also played a big role. The drive toward privatization, deregulation and free markets, which took off under Ronald Reagan and continued through the administrations of Bill Clinton and George W. Bush, has boosted the size and number of personal fortunes. Monetary and fiscal policy has also favored risk-taking and heavy borrowing by both consumers and companies.

Tax policy over the past 40 years has shifted heavily in favor of the wealthy, allowing them to keep more of their incomes and liquidity events. The top federal income tax rate has fallen from 91 percent in 1963 to 35 percent for 2007. The top tax rate on long-term capital gains—profits from selling stocks, bonds and other financial assets—has fallen to 15 percent from 20 percent over the past five years. The top rate on most dividends now is 15 percent, down from 38.6 percent in 2002.

The Tax Policy Center estimates that 80 percent of the tax savings from the Bush tax cuts went to the top 10 percent of taxpayers. Almost one-fifth of the benefits went to the top one-tenth of 1 percent. Efforts by Republicans, encouraged by several Old Money families, to repeal the estate tax would be a further boon for the rich, since the tax applies only to estates larger than $2 million.

The Third Wave has also had its share of fraudulent wealth creation, or what Harvard professor William Z. Ripley referred to in the Roaring Twenties as "prestidigitation, double-shuffling, honey-fugling, hornswoggling and skulduggery." The scandals at Enron, Worldcom, Adelphia Communications and Tyco uncovered systemic abuses in the way companies posted impressive earnings and stellar pay for their chiefs. The recent options-timing scandal—in which more than 100 companies are under scrutiny for their stock awards to executives who are giving them bigger profits—shows that corporate executives played by different rules from other investors when it came to their stock awards.

All these factors—the river of money, new technologies, globalization and market-friendly governments—have come together to create a new generation of rich people. They have made more money, more quickly, from more sources than any previous generation of wealth. As a result, Richistanis have redefined the way people become wealthy in America. They've also redefined the very meaning of the word "rich."

How Much Is "Rich"?

To make it into the top 1 percent of Americans, as measured by net worth, you need a net worth of $6 million. That's twice the level required in 1995. To get on the Forbes 400 list of richest Americans, you have to be a billionaire. The entry price was only $418 million in 1995.

For ages, the term "millionaire" was synonymous with "rich." Today, $1 million barely gets you a two-bedroom in Manhattan, let alone a place in the Hamptons. The wealth boom has created such a huge disconnect between Richistanis and the rest of the country that they now have dramatically different definitions of the term "rich."

Most Americans think $1 million would make them rich. How else to explain all those bestselling books such as *The Instant Millionaire* and *The Millionaire Next Door* and watching TV shows like *How to Be a Millionaire* and *Joe Millionaire?*

Yet in Richistan, $1 million just gets you in the door. Being a millionaire (or a millionaire household) has become almost common, since there are now more than nine million of them. Chock Full O'Nuts coffee, once the blue-collar favorite in New York, used to air a jingle that ended with the line: "Better coffee a millionaire's money can't buy." The new jingle ends with the line: "Better coffee a billionaire's money can't buy."

Wealth, in short, has been defined up because of all these Richistanis. So what's the new cutoff?

A study by PNC Advisors, a wealth-management firm, shows a surprising pattern among Richistanis when they're asked how much money would make them secure. They almost always answer that the amount they need to feel secure is *twice* their current level of net worth or income. Those worth $500,000 to $1 million said they needed $2.4 million. Those worth $1 million to $1.49 million said $3 million. And those with $10 million or more said $18 million. In other words, people's definition of "rich" is subjective and is usually twice their current net worth.

There are other, more objective benchmarks for what counts as "rich" today. To get into most private banks and trust companies today you need at least $10 million in investible assets. Some banks, like J.P. Morgan, require minimums of $25 million. Even then, you may not get VIP treatment; at Citigroup Private Bank, only clients with $100 million or more get into its Private Capital Partner's Group, which offers more lucrative deals and better investments. Let's say for now, however, that $10 million is the entry price for being rich in the eyes of those who manage money.

Another benchmark is investment returns. For many, the definition of "rich" means the ability to live comfortably off the income from your investments without dipping into your actual fortune. So if you have $1 million, and you make 5 percent a year from your investments, you would earn $50,000 a year. Most financial advisers say that today's rich need incomes of at least $500,000 to $1 million to live an upscale lifestyle, what with private school, a vacation home, maids, nannies and the like. That would require a fortune of at least $10 million, or probably more like $20 million. It's not huge, by today's standards. But it's enough to lead a comfortable life in Lower or Middle Richistan. (Later, we'll see exactly how much today's rich spend every year.)

For the purposes of this book, let's say that true wealth begins at somewhere around $10 million. Now, let's meet some Richistanis who have made—and lost—far greater amounts.

3

MAKING IT

Ed Bazinet, King of the Ceramic Village

One of the defining characteristics of Richistan is its diversity. Almost anyone, anywhere can make a fortune today with the right idea. The river of cash flowing around the world is so large that it's spilled into areas of the economy that most of us have never even heard of. For all the talk of flashy dot-commers, celebrities and Wall Streeters, many of today's Richistanis made their money from arcane, oddball products.

Take Sydell Miller. The most prominent socialite in Palm Beach, Ms. Miller is a Cleveland native who ran a hair salon with her husband until she came up with a new line of shampoo called Matrix Essentials. She sold the business to Bristol-Myers Squibb for $1 billion and now lives in a 30,000-square-foot home with its own ice-cream parlor.

James Leprino, a Denver-based cheese maker, helped create a new kind of mozzarella cheese that had the ideal melting properties for pizza, making it the top seller to Pizza Hut, Domino's and other big chains. Now he's worth more than $1 billion, and he just made the Forbes list.

Californian entrepreneur Aurelio F. Barreto III made tens of millions from a creation he called the Dogloo—an igloo-shaped doghouse—after he sold the business to an investment firm. Paul Cherrie, a candy maven, helped orchestrate a comeback for candy maker Dubble Bubble and sold it to Tootsie Roll Industries for nearly $200 million. Food tycoon Christopher Goldsbury made more than $1 billion from salsa, after selling the Pace salsa business to Campbell Soup.

Richistan is filled with masters of the banal who have turned everyday businesses into prized investments. Counted among today's elite are the pioneer of public storage (Bradley Wayne Hughes), the raja of roofing supplies (John Menard) and the potentate of potatoes (J. R. Simplot). They include, quite literally, the butchers (like Arkansas's billionaire Tyson family), bakers (Ohio's Schwebel family) and candlestick makers (Mike Kittredge of Yankee Candle, worth several hundred million).

Huge wealth can also come in small packages. While most people have heard of Ty Warner—the multibillionaire creator of Beanie Babies—few people have ever heard of the equally surprising fortune made by a folksy midwesterner named Ed Bazinet.

It Takes a Village

Ed Bazinet is one of the most wholesome businessmen you could meet. He's a stout, soft-spoken Catholic from rural Minnesota with a white beard, smiling eyes and round glasses. In his khakis, loafers and flannel shirts, Ed looks like a college professor or corner bookstore owner. At 63, he spends most of his days shuffling around his Manhattan penthouse, collecting art, running his charity and doting over his two prized ocicats, Nicolas and Nathan, who sleep under a heat lamp by his desk.

Ed Bazinet is worth more than $100 million. And when people ask him how he made it, he just says, "Imports."

"I'm not sure people would really understand," he says. "And if they did, they might not believe me."

That's because Bazinet made his fortune from miniature ceramic villages.

It all started at a plant nursery in Eden Prairie, Minnesota. Bazinet grew up in a working-class German family, and his father worked for the state water department. He went to a strict Catholic school and then to the University of Minnesota, pursuing his interest in arts and photography. In the middle of his sophomore year, he dropped out.

"I was more interested in working and business," he says.

He got a job at Bachman's, a giftware and plant shop, designing flower arrangements. He worked his way up to the gift department, and later started traveling to New York and Europe to buy up unique salad bowls, dinner trays and decorative figurines. Other retailers liked his products so much that he started selling wholesale. His first big hits were plant holders from Italy.

"It really clicked with the whole indoor-plant boom of the '70s," he says. "One of my innovations was putting the holders on wheels so people could move them around."

In 1971, he got a visit from an elderly St. Louis–based potter who sold vases and jars from the back of his truck. At the end of his sales pitch, the potter showed Ed a special creation—a cookie jar shaped like a little Victorian house. The house was hand-painted in intricate colors and had tiny puffs of white snow on the roof, made with a special glaze.

Ed loved it. The piece was so detailed that it transported him to another world.

"It was just a little piece of ceramic, but it was very exciting. It was nostalgic."

Bazinet asked the potter if he could make some changes, like cutting holes in the windows and installing a light so it would glow like a real house at night.

The potter frowned.

"Then it wouldn't be a cookie jar," he said.

"Well, we could call it a night-light," Bazinet said.

The potter agreed to give it a try. He and Ed made six other versions of the Victorian night-lights and put them on the Bachman's sales shelf just before Christmas. They priced them at a hefty $150 to $200 each, thinking they would never sell. They sold out instantly.

Ed realized he was on to something big. But he knew the St. Louis potter, with his fading health and single kiln, wouldn't be able to keep up with bigger orders. So Ed packed his bags and flew to Taiwan.

In the early 1970s, global sourcing was still in its infancy. Finding a ceramics factory in Taiwan that could make hand-painted Victorian-house night-lights with puffs of snow wasn't easy. Eventually, he found a factory that was willing to give it a try, and he spent the next three years overseeing production. He spent hours and hours on the plant floor, teaching the factory workers how to paint the tiny shutters and getting the roof shingles just so.

"I'm a micromanager," Ed says. "When the workers heard me coming, they would all try to hide."

By the mid-1970s, he was selling thousands of tiny houses a year. He formed a new company called Department 56, which had been the in-house name for Bachman's giftware department. Ed owned 20 percent of the company, and the Bachman family owned the rest.

Ed came up with a novel idea. Instead of getting people to buy one or two Victorian night-lights, why not get them to buy 10 or 12? People could buy entire villages of night-lights.

"The innovation was turning these houses into a scene, a real village," he said.

Ed did most of the designs himself. He created miniature ceramic fire stations, post offices, schools, train stations and stores. He built tiny pet stores, barbershops, car dealerships, diners, toy stores and even a snow-covered trailer park. He did licensing deals and made a Coca-Cola bottling plant and Budweiser brewery. One of his favorites was the NFL stadium. "That was complicated, and pretty tough to build," he says.

"We didn't do funeral homes or cemeteries. But we did have churches, every kind of church. We even made a synagogue, but that didn't sell too well."

All the buildings had a cozy, New England feel, like

something Norman Rockwell would make, if he had made ceramic villages. Bazinet called his first series the Snow Village. That was followed by the Dickens Village (modeled after 19th-century Britain), the Christmas in the City series, and the North Pole series, which included the popular Elfin Snow-Cone House and Reindeer Flight School.

An entire new industry was born. Department 56 soon had its own group of fanatical collectors, who set up their villages as Christmas displays. Some customers filled up giant tables and entire rooms of their homes with Department 56 scenes, requiring the company to design specialized electrical strips and installation equipment. Many of the customers lived in the suburbs of Florida and California—snowbirds who missed the winter wonderlands and small towns of their youth. Yet they were all devoted Department 56 customers. They became like Star Trek fans, holding their own conventions and trade shows, and anxiously awaiting news on the latest village designs.

"It wasn't just a mom thing, because the dad had to get involved to build the display and the kids would each get to pick out a new building every Christmas," Ed said. "So it really spread. It became a tradition with many of these families."

Sales soared from $250,000 the first year to more than $100 million by the 1980s. Ed ran almost every aspect of the business, even after it grew to 120 employees. He flew to Taiwan to oversee manufacturing, sold to retailers, negotiated licensing deals and oversaw all the product design. Every Friday night, he took home stacks of letters from customers expressing their profound joy at receiving the latest Dickens Village Bob Cratchit Cottage or North Pole Yummy Gummy Gumdrop Factory.

"It was like these people were having emotional experiences over a tiny ceramic building," Ed says. "It was amazing. I myself couldn't really understand it."

By the early 1990s, Ed was making more than $750,000 a year, and he made another $1 million from a separate transaction with the company. The money, however, wasn't fulfilling.

"I know it's hard for some people to understand," he says. "But I'm not money motivated. For me it was all about my product line and having success with that product that was in high demand. It was about selling to the right stores. I'm a merchant at heart."

By the early 1990s, Bazinet was growing tired of it all. He was working 18-hour days, seven days a week, and spent most of his life on airplanes. He even grew tired of the customers. After reading thousands of glowing tributes to Department 56, he had a special rubber stamp made with the words "Get a Life." Ed would stamp the words on the most effusive letters before sending them to customer service. The phrase became his hallmark at the company, and he started referring to some of his customers as the "Get a Life crowd."

Bazinet and the Bachmans decided to sell. They didn't want to go public, since Ed hated all the badgering and second-guessing from shareholders. So they shopped the firm around Wall Street and eventually settled on a deal with the buyout shop Forstmann Little. Theodore "Teddy" Forstmann, the famously coiffed, outspoken buyout king, was better known for collecting supermodels than for miniature ceramics. Yet he knew good cash flow when he saw it, and Department 56 was spinning off piles of cash, with $172 million in annual sales. Forstmann Little bought the business for about $270 million. Bazinet netted more than $50 million from his stake and other considerations and reinvested a portion back into the business.

He agreed to stay on as CEO, since Forstmann Little assured him they wouldn't take the company public anytime soon. Less than a year later, they told Bazinet they were taking it public. Ed went on the road with Goldman Sachs to pitch the company to investors, a job he dreaded. He had to answer endless questions about his products and business, which no one outside the "Get a Life crowd" could really understand. Big pension funds, money managers and investors had a hard time understanding how miniature ceramic villages would be the next hot growth industry.

Paul Laufer, an analyst with Principal Financial Securities, said one institutional investor asked, "How many fat old ladies in Milwaukee were there to buy [the houses]?" Bazinet recalls a 20-something portfolio manager in Denver asking if he was selling "toy houses." "I was ready to reach across the table and smack him."

The offering was a huge success. Ed netted another $100 million in stock sales. This time, he wanted out. The offering had sapped his enthusiasm for the business, and he was still spending most of his time on airplanes. The final straw was a long flight from Hawaii to Minnesota in 1992. Ed was a chain-smoker and the Hawaii flight marked the first day of the smoking ban on aircraft. "I asked the flight attendant in first class what she would do if I lit up and she said the pilot would touch down at the nearest airport and have me arrested," he said. "I decided not to test them."

Ed told Forstmann he was quitting. After begging and pleading, they made him an offer he couldn't refuse—his own private jet. Forstmann owned Gulfstream and, despite a long waiting list for jets, they freed up a G2 formerly owned by the Wrigley gum family and sold it to Department 56 for Ed to use.

"It was very clever. They could have offered me a million-dollar raise and I would have said no. But a jet? Wow. Every time I stepped onto the plane I felt like a kid walking into a candy store. I never quite got over it."

Mostly because of the jet, Ed stayed on another five years, driving sales to more than $240 million a year. When the office politics and boardroom dramas got to be too much, he finally retired in 1997.

Getting a Life

When you walk into Ed's Manhattan penthouse today, you won't find any signs of Department 56. There are no snow villages on the mantle, or Lucite "deal trophies" on his desk commemorating his convertible-bond offerings, as with most entrepreneurs. His only "ceramic collection" to speak of is a cabinet full of French antique models of human heads, once used for medical studies.

"I just liked the way they looked," Ed smiles. "I find them artistic."

Indeed, Bazinet's 10,000-square-foot glass and chrome palace looks more like a wing of the Museum of Modern Art than a home, with a giant Gerhard Richter painting, a bulbous chrome sculpture by Anish Kapoor and a 700-piece chandelier by glass artist Dale Chihuly. All the rooms are ultraminimalist, with gleaming white surfaces, flat-screen TVs and dark wood furniture.

"I had a real-estate agent in here the other day looking over the place and he counted 13 plasma screens in the house," he said. "I didn't believe it, but then I counted, and he was right. I didn't even realize."

The house contains only one physical reminder of his old life. Hanging on a wall next to his secretary is a blue neon sign that reads "Get a life!" It was modeled after his old rubber stamp.

Yet getting a life after making so much wealth hasn't been easy for Bazinet. Like most Richistanis, he devoted his life to building his company, and when he left, he also left behind a big part of his identity. He is addicted to projects—and once they're done, he often loses interest.

"It's my personality," he says. "I get consumed by projects."

Take his penthouse. Ed spent three years and millions of dollars renovating the five-story showplace, which is one of the most elaborate in downtown Manhattan. He oversaw the construction of every molding, window and fixture. He had the stairs—a swirling tower of stainless steel, glass and Venetian porcelain—hand-carved by local artisans. He commissioned special artworks, like the 30-foot-tall LED sculpture by the artist Jenny Holzer, which hangs near the stairs.

Now that the house is finished, however, Ed sees the penthouse as one big hassle. He's suing his former contractor and now spends hours a day on the phone with lawyers. He's confounded by the home's state-of-the-art lighting and security system, which is operated by several remote computer servers. One afternoon, he shows me a tiny scratch on the glass stairwell that was left by one of the installers.

"Most people wouldn't notice it," he says. "But I see it and it drives me crazy."

There also are problems with the space itself. Simply put, Ed says it's too big. He lives there with his partner—a Belgian photographer—and their two cats. They rarely use many of the rooms.

"It's not comfortable," he says. "Sometimes you don't know until you're living in a space. But this feels too big for two people. It's great when you have people over for a party. But upstairs it feels like a big fishbowl with just a few people. There are no cozy areas."

So Ed has put the house on the market through Sotheby's. The asking price: $28.5 million.

The sale is part of what Ed hopes will be a new, simpler phase of his life. After accumulating so much wealth, and so many things, he's decided to downsize. He's selling off his beach house in Puerto Vallarta, along with an antique biwing plane that he kept at his Montana ranch to give aerial tours to friends and family.

He's tired of all the bills, lawsuits, negotiations and upkeep that go along with having multiple homes and projects. Every Friday, for instance, he sorts through "the pile," a stack of mail that's several inches high, mostly solicitations and invitations to fund-raisers and benefits.

"Part of my frustration is that I feel busier now than I've ever been. But I don't have the results or rewards like I used to." He adds, "In the end I made a lot of money. But there are two sides to the coin, good and bad."

So after selling his New York apartment, Ed plans to move into a smaller place. He hopes to spend part of the year at his ranch in Montana, getting healthy, relaxing and trying to enjoy life more. And he plans to focus more and more on his foundation, which supports the environment, children's crisis centers, scholarships and other causes in Minnesota.

"I have trouble relaxing," he says. "But I'm learning."

There is one luxury, however, that he couldn't live without: the jet. After leaving Department 56, he bought part ownership in a Gulfstream, which he used to travel to Europe, Africa and his ranch on Montana. He decided to sell it because he started feeling guilty about the expense.

"Maybe it's my midwestern personality. I just kept thinking that was money I could be spending for kids' charity or something else."

In 2005, after enduring the hassles of commercial flights and the expense of charters, he wanted the plane back. So he recently purchased another Gulfstream with a partner.

"It's still hard to believe," he says, shaking his head. "Me . . . owning a jet."

BAZINET isn't alone. Even as today's Richistanis make more money than they could have ever imagined, and buy all the baubles they could want, they're having a hard time enjoying their success. They're too young to retire, too driven to relax and too concerned with keeping up with the next guy to live the storied life of leisure. In today's Richistan, even billionaires are rarely content.

4

LIVING IT

Tim Blixseth

Just before dawn, Tim Blixseth is standing on the deck of his 157-foot yacht in his bathrobe.

"Where the hell am I?" he asks, rubbing his eyes, somewhere off the coast of Mexico. "I've been waking up in a different place every day this week. I feel like a vagabond."

"Vagabond" is a relative term when you're traveling with Tim Blixseth. On Sunday morning, he woke up in his 3,000-square-foot cabin at the Yellowstone Club, a private golf-and-ski club that Blixseth founded in the Montana Rockies. The next day he woke up at a luxury lodge on a 3,200-acre fishing ranch near Cody, Wyoming.

Monday night, it was back home, "home" also being a relative term. Blixseth and his wife, Edra, live on a 240-acre spread near Palm Springs, California, that makes most five-star resorts look puny by comparison. The estate, called Porcupine Creek, has a 30,000-square-foot mansion, 12 guest cottages—each the size of a single-family home—a full-service spa, two swimming pools, an amphitheater and an underground ballroom. For their backyard, the Blixseths built a private, 19-hole golf course (with clubhouse) that golf experts rank as one of the best in the country. The estate grounds are carpeted with emerald-green grass, fountains, burbling streams, waterfalls and more than a million exotic flowers—all the more remarkable for being in the middle of the desert.

On Tuesday morning, Tim and Edra boarded their Gulfstream 550 and flew to Manzaneo, Mexico, just south of Puerto Vallarta. There, they jumped on their yacht and motored to Tamarindo—a secluded jungle resort that Tim recently purchased. Two days later, it was off to Tahiti to another Blixseth resort playground.

"Not a bad life," he says, sipping chardonnay on his yacht during sunset. "I wish my dad could only see me now."

On its face, Tim Blixseth's life looks like one long, luxurious vacation. And in some ways, it is. After making millions in the timber business, Blixseth retired at the age of 40 and tried living the Good Life. But when his plans for a family retreat in Montana caught on with friends, he launched a second career building high-end resorts. Now he's a billionaire, with his Yellowstone Club and Yellowstone Club World becoming two of the most popular playgrounds for the superrich.

And that's just a side business. Blixseth buys and sells land, and owns more than 500,000 acres of property in the

United States and Mexico. He day-trades stocks, funds start-up companies, runs his own charitable foundation, develops real estate, operates his own music label and writes pop songs.

Blixseth is so busy that he tends to forget that he officially "retired" more than 15 years ago.

"As you can tell," Tim says, racing around his golf course one afternoon in his high-speed cart, "I have trouble sitting still."

The New Leisure Class

Tim Blixseth is a leading member of the new overachieving overclass. Like Ed Bazinet and many of today's Richistanis, Blixseth has all the trappings of the life of leisure— multiple vacation homes, planes, boats and cars. And he's got enough money to last generations. Yet Tim has little time to enjoy it.

He's always building a new home, launching new companies and sketching out new business plans on his dinner napkins. He's a serial entrepreneur and project addict, always looking for the next big problem to solve and industry to reinvent. He bounds up stairs two at a time, fidgets in his chair and rarely sleeps in the same house (or boat or jet) two nights in a row. He fires off e-mails at 3 A.M. and keeps his drivers and pilots in a constant state of panic as they try to keep up with his daily movements. (You can always hear Tim approaching because of the urgent beeps and shouts from his staffers' radios.)

Blixseth and his kind are reinventing the leisure class. The idle rich are being replaced by the workaholic wealthy.

They don't have the time or patience to putter around the croquet court or sip away the hours in the polo box like Old Money. In an economy driven more than ever by competition and innovation, the people who succeed tend to be those who thrive on risk, reinvention and brutal hours. Richistanis are younger than the rich of the past, and far more likely to be working or running their own businesses. They climbed their way up from the middle class and continue to define themselves by their 18-hour days and outsized productivity.

For Richistanis, work has become their play, and play has become their work. Yachts and jets are now loaded with communications gear to allow the rich to keep working even if they're floating in the Mediterranean or soaring above the Atlantic. The new crowd in Palm Beach, as we'll see in a later chapter, spends as much time on their laptops as they do on the golf course. When I asked a hedge-fund manager in Greenwich whether he'd joined a local yacht or country club, he replied, "And do what? Sit around in white pants and a blue blazer and complain about the government? Not for me."

Blixseth typifies this new ideal of working leisure. *Forbes* magazine recently ranked Blixseth as one of the 400 richest Americans, putting his net worth at about $1.2 billion. Yet he looks nothing like a billionaire, at least in the traditional sense. His daily uniform consists of a pair of cargo shorts, Hawaiian shirts, sandals and a base-ball cap. He has a perpetual tan, scruffy goatee, buzz-cut brown hair and wiry physique, making him look more like a surf-shop manager than a timber tycoon. He carries three things in his pocket—a wad of cash, a pen and a $3 plastic calculator. When Tim has important meetings with bankers or CEO types, he'll sometimes wear a button-down shirt and long pants. Suits are out. "I only wear them a few times a year. And that's if I have weddings or funerals."

Tim looks so downscale that he's frequently kicked out of high-end stores and car dealerships. One day, dressed in muddy work boots and jeans, he took his son, Beau, to a men's boutique near Palm Springs to buy a graduation suit. The salesman headed them off at the door and said, "I think you'd be better off at the mall."

"You should have seen the look on that guy's face when we drove away in the Rolls," he says.

Tim loves pranks. One day when I accompanied him to Mexico, he conspired with Mexican immigration to have me briefly detained for "smuggling." (He had the officials laughing for hours.) He and Edra throw epic parties; for Tim's 50th birthday, they turned their golf course into a living timeline, installing a '50s diner on their driving range, complete with classic cars. They set up similar stations for the '60s, '70s, '80s and '90s and finished with a "time tunnel" that ushered guests to a spaceship that released a giant birthday cake. Former president Gerald Ford sent birthday wishes via video. For Edra's 50th, Tim hired an entire cast of Munchkins from a *Wizard of Oz* production and had Paul Anka sing a personalized version of "My Way."

For one of their wedding anniversaries, Tim set up dinner for two by their pool. On the table, he placed a crystal bowl filled with 50 raw carrots. When Edra asked why they were there, Tim said, "Count them," and underneath she found a 50-carat diamond necklace.

Still, Tim likes to portray himself as a kind of Everyman's

Billionaire—just a poor preacher's son who made good in the timber trade. He grew up in Roseburg, Oregon, a small logging town 185 miles south of Portland. His father couldn't support the family because of a heart condition so they lived off welfare. Tim also helped out by working the night shift at a local sawmill.

"I was born with a rusty spoon in my mouth," he says. (He still has an aversion to Spam, which his family got for free and ate regularly.)

Growing up poor, Tim developed something of a chip on his shoulder. In junior high school, students waited in two lines in the cafeteria: the "paying" line or the "free-lunch" line for welfare kids. Tim had to wait in the free line and was constantly badgered by other kids.

"They'd point at me and yell 'welfare kid, welfare kid!,'" he says. "Boy, that really got me seething."

Tim got his first lesson in success from his high school shop teacher.

"The guy's name was Wally Eichler. Everyone called him Rough Cut Wally, because he was one of these real tough, no-nonsense guys. On the first day of class, Rough Cut Wally said to us, 'I don't give a damn if you learn a single thing in this class. But just remember that you can do anything you want in this country if you want to. You can succeed or fail, but it's up to you. You're entirely responsible.'" Blixseth took the advice to heart and made a perfectly crafted tin box that he still keeps in his dressing room to remind him of Wally.

Despite being a preacher's son, Blixseth placed little faith in religion. His parents joined a Christian cult led by a man who claimed that the group's 167 members would be the only people admitted to heaven.

"It seemed ridiculous to me that only these 167 people would get into heaven," Tim says. "Why only those 167 people?"

At the age of 15, Blixseth decided to go into business. He was combing the classified ads in the local paper one day and noticed an ad for three donkeys that were being sold for $25 each. He took his savings, bought the donkeys and brought them home. The next day, he put an ad in the paper offering "three pack mules" for $75 each. They sold instantly.

"I wasn't selling 'donkeys.' I was selling 'pack mules,'" he says. "That's how I learned about marketing."

Soon after, he saw an ad in the paper for a 360-acre piece of timber property for $90,000. Tim barely had $1,000 to his name. Yet he bought the property with $1,000 down and a promise to pay the rest within a week.

"The realtor said to me, 'Kid, I'm going to take your money to teach you a lesson. If you don't pay me the rest of the $90,000 within a week, I'm going to keep your $1,000.'"

Yet Tim found a timber company to buy the property a week later for $140,000, giving him an instant profit of $50,000.

"My dad assumed I must have done something illegal since it was so much money," he said. "He was going to turn me in to the police until I explained the whole thing."

Blixseth launched a career as a timberland trader. He combed through land records in remote towns in the Pacific Northwest, bought overlooked properties, and flipped them to logging companies or larger landowners. Later, he branched out into logging and milling. By the time he was 30, he was earning $1 million a month. He met Edra, a successful hotelier, married, bought a large home and started raising their four kids (all from previous marriages).

Then, in the early 1980s, it all came crashing down. Timber prices plunged by more than 80 percent. Blixseth was highly leveraged and was forced to declare bankruptcy. He lost his business, sold the house and struggled for months to pay the light bills.

"It was the best thing that ever happened to me," he says. "I learned to never again have any debt. Debt is the thing that kills you."

To this day, Blixseth doesn't have a single mortgage on his homes. The bankruptcy, and his poor childhood, are also the main reasons Tim likes buying land—and always with cash. "No one can take it away from me. It's permanent."

After bankruptcy, Blixseth went back to land trading and eventually built up enough cash to team up with a partner to form Crown-Pacific, a timber and paper company. He sold his stake in 1990 for more than $20 million and retired at age 40.

"I thought $20 million was all I could ever need for the rest of my life," he says.

He bought a Citation jet and a home in Sun River, Oregon. He kicked back and returned to his first love—singing and songwriting. In the 1970s, Blixseth had become a minor pop sensation with a song called "I Hope to Find Your Rainbow" while another one of his tunes, "Coyote Ugly," became a cult college hit.

After a few months, Tim realized he wasn't cut out for retirement. He needed projects, deals and problems to solve.

"He was miserable," Edra recalls. "So were we."

In 1991, Tim bought 164,000 acres of land in Montana from another timber company and orchestrated a complex swap with the federal government. In exchange for 37,000 acres of environmentally sensitive land (it was a breeding area for elk and grizzly bears), the government granted Tim's company about 13,500 acres of more accessible and more commercially attractive land on the northwest corner of Yellowstone National Park, near Big Sky resort. Because of its size and importance, the deal required special approval from Congress. (Tim is a generous donor to Republican and Democratic politicians.)

Initially, Tim and Edra planned to use the property for a private family ranch. But one day, they were having a picnic on the property and Tim looked up at a nearby mountain slope and said, "Why don't we put a ski lift there?"

"We thought it would be a nice little retreat for our family and friends," Tim says.

So many friends wanted to join them that they decided to turn it into a private ski-and-golf community. Thus, the Yellowstone Club was born. The club has nearly 300 members, each of whom pays $250,000 to join along with millions of dollars to build or buy a house on the site. Bill Gates is a member, along with News Corp. president Peter Chernin, Comcast president Steve Burke, and former U.S. vice president Dan Quayle. As the club's Web site says, "Sometimes you have to pay to play."

When Tim started Yellowstone, resort owners and vacation experts said he was crazy. People would never pay that much to join a club, especially since they could already ski and golf on their own in Aspen and other upscale locales. One friend asked if he also believed in the "tooth fairy." Hence, Tim's named his new $20 million yacht "Tooth Fairy."

Being rich themselves, Tim and Edra know exactly what other wealthy people want. Security at the Yellowstone Club is tight and is led by a former Secret Service agent to President Ford. Members can ski more than 60 trails without having to wait in lift lines or dodge the hoi polloi. On the golf course, tee times are unheard-of. Legions of club staff are always on hand to prewarm the members' ski boots, stock their homes with groceries and flowers and, in one case, hand-slice special meat for their dogs.

Indeed, the big draw of the Yellowstone Club is the comfort of knowing that everyone around you is wealthy.

"People can relax and be themselves," Edra says. "They can let their kids run around without worrying about them."

By 2005, however, Tim was getting restless again. He needed a new project. One day, a Yellowstone member asked him about destination clubs, in which members pay six-figure annual dues to stay at upscale vacation homes. Tim and Edra liked the idea so much they decided to create their own, but on a much grander scale.

Using hundreds of millions of dollars of their own money, they went on a global shopping spree to find the most exotic and private escapes in the world. "They had to be places that even the wealthy can't find or afford on their own," as Tim puts it. "They had to have the wow factor. Or more like the double wow factor."

They bought a plot of land near St. Andrews, Scotland— the legendary home of golf—where they're building a golf course ringed by luxury cottages. They bought a 13th-century castle outside Paris, restored with an indoor swimming pool, full-service spa and chef's kitchen. They scooped up a plush lodge and trout-fishing lake near Cody, Wyoming, along with property in the California desert to build a spa. They purchased three beach retreats—Tamarindo in Mexico, a private island in Turks and Caicos and a resort in Tahiti.

To make it easier for guests to get around, Tim threw in two yachts and a fleet of private jets. And he hired an army of staffers, from wine experts and chefs to butlers and concierges.

"You might start off taking the jet to St. Andrews for some golf," Tim says. "Then you fly to the French castle for a few days, then do some yachting around the Mediterranean for a few days before heading back to the U.S. It's exactly what I would want in a vacation."

Not that he's ever vacationed at his resorts. When I asked Tim and Edra if they can remember their last non-working holiday, they pause.

"I think 1999, so seven years ago," Tim says.

"No," Edra says. "We worked during that one."

The Conflicted Elite

For all his wealth, Tim Blixseth hates being labeled "rich." Rich people, he says, are stuffy, pretentious and out of touch. Richistanis like to think of themselves as ordinary people, albeit with extraordinary fortunes. They go out of their way to appear normal. Richistanis wear polo shirts, casual slacks and open-collar dress shirts, forsaking the old uniform of monogrammed shirts and suits. As one

Palm Beacher told me: "Suits are for the people who work for me." Richistanis describe themselves as "down to earth," even as they take off in their private Gulfstreams. As the billionaire vulture investor David Tepper told *The Wall Street Journal* recently, "I'm just a middle-class dad trapped in a rich man's body."

Blixseth is equally disparaging of the "rich."

"I don't like most rich people," he says. "They can be arrogant."

Wealth, he adds, can bring out the worst—or best—in people, making them a more exaggerated version of themselves.

"Money is like a truth serum. It brings out people's true nature. So if someone's already a jerk, they become more of a jerk after they're rich."

When I remind him that he's a billionaire, he says: "When people say that, I think they're talking about someone else. Billion is a number that seems so far on the horizon it doesn't even sound real to me."

The confusion is common among today's Richistanis. They strive to maintain their middle-class identities. These aren't the yuppie, bourgeois bohemians that David Brooks brilliantly described in *Bobos in Paradise;* Richistanis are much wealthier and more extravagant. Blixseth and other Richistanis have dual personalities, with middle-class values and upper-class lifestyles.

Every morning (or at least on those mornings when he's home), Blixseth wakes up early, gets in his Nissan Armada and drives to the local Starbucks. He orders his usual café mocha, finds a chair and sits down to read the paper. With a private kitchen staff of 10 cooks—including an award-winning German chef—Tim could easily find coffee at home. Yet he prefers to be around regular people.

"It keeps me sane," he says on a recent morning, sandwiched at a Starbucks table between a screaming baby and a group of octogenarian retirees.

Tim's split personality is reflected even more clearly in his choice of cars. I ask him one afternoon how many cars he owns. He starts counting, runs out of fingers and says, "I really don't know."

He once walked into a Bentley dealership and bought a $250,000 convertible on impulse. When I notice two gleaming Rolls-Royce Phantoms—one painted in two-tone black and silver and the other blue—parked at the back of his house, I ask him why he needs two. (They each retail for more than $320,000.)

"The two-tone one, that's my restaurant car. You get a better parking space [from the valets]."

At the same time, he recently phased out his family's fleet of Range Rovers for Nissan Armadas. They were, Tim boasts, half the price.

"A great deal," he says. "I paid half as much for a car that's just as good or better than the Range Rovers. Why should I pay more?"

He then offers to show me his favorite car. Bypassing the two Rolls, he walks over to a tiny, 1,600-pound Smart Car, which retails for $20,000 and gets sixty miles per gallon.

"I love it. Sixty miles per gallon, isn't that great?"

At the same time, Blixseth's lifestyle is expanding so quickly he sometimes loses track. One night over dinner, I ask Tim and Edra how many house staff they employ at Porcupine Creek.

"With the maids, security guys, spa staff, kitchen and everything," Tim says, "probably about 60 or 70."

Edra interrupts. "It's more than that."

"More?" Tim asks.

"It's 105," she says

"If it's 105 we have a problem," Tim says.

"I just counted yesterday. It's 105."

"Then we have a problem," Tim says, smiling as if it's really not a problem.

Porcupine Creek is one of the most lavish estates in the country. The wooden gates open up onto a Disney-esque fantasy, with flowers, waterfalls, golf greens and private roads lit with French streetlamps that once lined the Champs Élysées.

A soaring fountain, modeled after Las Vegas's Bellagio, rises in front of the main house, a two-story Mediterra-nean palace. Inside is a menagerie of 18th-century European antiques, oversized fish tanks, mosaics, crystal chande-liers, Asian sculptures, art deco bars, carved-wood ceilings and giant birdcages.

The Blixseths' bed came from the archbishop of Milan's quarters and has a carved Jesus on one side (Tim's) and a Mary on the other (Edra's). Their walk-in refrigerator is bigger than most New York apartments.

Their house even has its own logo, which adorns the towels in every bathroom and the shirts on every staffer. The Blixseths' dogs are equally jet set: Their shih tzus were named Learjet and G2. (They're planning an up-grade to a G550.)

At the same time, Tim and Edra give away millions each year to philanthropy. And Tim's giving style is uni-que, to say the least. When he reads about someone in the paper who's suffering or in need, he shows up with gifts and cash. The element of surprise is key, making him a kind of guerrilla philanthropist. In 2004, he read about a jobless, paraplegic man in California who was robbed of everything in his home. Blixseth pulled up the next morning with a truck full of new appliances, computers and electronic equipment. When he saw Tim standing at the front door, the man thought he was being robbed a second time.

"He peeked out the door and said 'Please go away. I don't have anything left.'" Tim recalls. "Eventually, after we started unloading the refrigerator and air conditioners, he let us in."

Tim also became a big force behind the Habitat for Humanity campaign for Katrina victims. He donated $2 million to the effort and got dozens of his wealthy friends and members to contribute as well. He also wrote a song, called "Heart of America," which was later recorded to help raise Katrina funds.

Around Palm Springs, Tim is known for handing out $20 bills to valets, busboys and Starbucks baristas. One day when we were in Mexico, he handed a $100 tip to the driver, who stared at Tim like he was crazy. When I asked him if he worried that the money would be wasted, Tim responded: "I hope he *does* waste it. If that driver takes that money and buys a cold beer, and sits on his porch and drinks that beer, and it's the only moment of real pleasure he has all day, then I've done a good thing. That's worth it to me."

One day, in the summer of 2006, I called Tim and asked how he was doing. "Great," he said. "I think I just made another billion dollars." A large real-estate developer wanted to build on a 4,200-acre piece of land that Tim owned in Southern Califoria, proposing a deal that could eventually net Tim $1 billion.

"It's true what they say—the first billion is the hardest. The second one was pretty easy."

So is losing a billion. At the end of 2006, Tim and Edra decided to divorce. They split their assets in half, through an amicable settlement, and Tim figures he's still worth about $1 billion after the split.

Yet in today's Richistan, divorce isn't the only way to lose a fortune. The increasingly volatile financial markets, while creating huge opportunies, have also created new risks for the wealthy.

5

LOSING IT

Pete Musser

Pete Musser remembers the moment he became a billionaire.

It was the week after Christmas in 1999. Pete, a 72-year-old entrepreneur, was relaxing with his 34-year-old girlfriend, Hilary Grinker, at the Las Ventanas resort in Los Cabos, the Mexican beach retreat. They were lounging next to their private pool overlooking the Sea of Cortez, when Pete called his secretary to check the stock price of his company, Safeguard Scientific. Pete was Safeguard's founder and he held millions of shares. Safeguard had become an investor in scores of dot-com companies, so its shares were soaring with the dot-com bubble. The day

Pete called, his share price broke $80. His other stocks, most of them dot-com companies, were also skyrocketing.

He and Hilary both did a quick calculation and smiled. Pete Musser was now worth more than a billion dollars.

Hilary started jumping up and down on the bed.

"Oh my God," she screamed. "What are we going to do with all of this money?!"

Not that they needed any suggestions. A few years earlier they had purchased a 24-acre estate in Bryn Mawr, Pennsylvania, called Bonfield, which had a 7,400-square-foot mansion, 6,800-square-foot guesthouse, indoor tennis court, indoor pool, fully equipped gym and sprawling gardens. Hilary filled the house with antiques from Europe, along with hand-painted murals.

They also bought land in Nantucket, where they built a plush summer home with "his" and "her" tennis courts. To get to all their real estate, they bought a Challenger jet and a stretch limousine. They vacationed at the Four Seasons in Nevis and acquired new wardrobes. Pete gave away millions to the Red Cross, United Way and Boy Scouts, becoming one of Pennsylvania's most celebrated philanthropists.

"Boy, did it feel great," Pete recalls. "Hilary certainly enjoyed it. And I enjoyed it, too. But the main thing I enjoyed was what we were doing for all the Safeguard shareholders who were seeing their investments go up. That's what really made me proud."

Until the spring of 2000. That's when the dot-com bubble burst, the markets tanked and Pete's stocks plummeted. In just a few months, he went from billionaire to debtor. Today, he has a negative net worth of $15 million, since he owes money to Safeguard from margin loans. After being ousted from the company, he works in a small office on the Safeguard campus.

He and Hilary, whom he married in 2000, have divorced. They laid off most of their staff and sold the plane, the land in Nantucket, and a place in the Poconos. Pete now lives alone at Bonfield, which he's put on the market for $8.5 million. He rambles around the giant house with his arthritic golden retriever, Higgins. When I visited one morning in May, the family room was still festooned with Christmas decorations, including an artificial tree decked out with lights and ornaments. Musser says he often wakes up in the morning, turns on the tree and just stares at the twinkling lights.

"It's cheery," he says, sitting with Higgins next to the tree. "It makes me feel better."

Fear of Falling

While the new rich can make giant fortunes in record time, they can lose them just as quickly. Financial markets and fast-changing technologies have created historic opportunities for entrepreneurs and corporate chiefs to make millions and billions virtually overnight. Yet they have also created historic opportunities to lose it all equally fast.

For Richistanis, this is the new Fear of Falling. While the bulk of the country's top wealth used to be grounded in hard assets, like land, real estate, trucks, factories and buildings, much of today's wealth is tethered to stocks, options, derivatives and other free-floating assets. As a consequence, Richistanis are more vulnerable than ever to sudden wealth shocks.

The stock-market declines of 2001 marked the biggest losses. American millionaires lost about $200 billion between 2001 and 2002. And it wasn't just 20-something dot-commers who had to move back to their parents' garages.

Of the 400 people on the 2001 Forbes list, 230 were not on the list in 1989. For every new entry on the list, a former member falls off, and it's almost always due to falling stock prices. The 2005 Forbes dropouts included Thomas Marsico, the mutual-fund magnate; Leon Levine of Family Dollar Stores; Norman W. Waitt Jr. of Gateway; Hollywood deal maker Jeffrey Katzenberg; and Little Caesars pizza king Michael Ilitch. Bill Gates lost $12 billion of his paper wealth in April of 2000, when a judge ruled that Microsoft had violated federal antitrust rules and Microsoft stock tanked. Paper wealth, after all, is just that.

Granted, Richistanis don't often descend into poverty. Studies show that when people tumble from the top of the wealth ladder—known as downward mobility—they usually land just a few rungs lower. What's more, many of today's rich start with such huge fortunes that even an 80 percent drop leaves them with plenty left over.

Still, today's rich are vulnerable to instant changes in their fortunes. In a research paper on wealth mobility, sociologist Thomas DiPrete wrote that a large number of today's top earners break into the ranks of the wealthy temporarily, only to fall back to their previous positions. In other words, income and wealth volatility—a problem usually associated with the middle class and lower middle class—has started creeping up the economic ladder.

"While a large proportion of any elite income groups resides in this (upper end) group on a more or less permanent basis, their ranks always include another large group that crosses the threshold only on a temporary basis, later to fall back to a lower income category."

Few falls have been as dramatic as Warren "Pete" Musser's. The Mussers don't like to talk about what they call "the troubles." And they've never discussed their experience publicly, saying they want to get on with their new lives.

"I always think about the future, not the past," says the ever-optimistic Musser.

Yet Pete's story is a surprising departure from all the other dot-com busts at the turn of the century. He wasn't a naïve, 20-something techie with a get-rich-quick plan. He was a gray-haired pillar of the Pennsylvania business establishment and a veteran businessman who spent nearly 50 years building successful start-up companies. In fact, it was the very same qualities that helped him in business—his unshakable optimism and faith in new markets—that eventually proved his undoing in the Internet age.

"I have no one to blame but myself," he says. "I got sucked in by the irresistible force of the Internet."

Musser's can-do drive served him well most of his life. Tall and slim, with bright blue eyes, a gravelly voice and a booming laugh, Musser looks the part of a folksy, old-school CEO. He's a popular figure around Philadelphia's Main Line, known for his bright yellow sweater vests, sporty convertibles and winning tennis game. He's a natural charmer; even at 80, he's dating frequently ("Some of these girls are in their 30s!" he says), though he admits many of his dates still assume he's wealthy.

"I don't exactly discourage them of the notion," he says.

He's equally persistent in business. Years ago, he was meeting with a potential business partner in South Carolina who mentioned that he liked tennis. Musser didn't have his tennis gear, but later that night, after a few cocktails, he agreed to play for two hours in his bare feet.

In his office, Musser keeps a bronze statue called "The Self-Made Man," which depicts a muscular Adonis with a chisel carving himself out of a rock base. "I identify with him," Musser says. "You make your own way in this world and you can be whoever you want to be."

Musser was raised by a single mom in Harrisburg, Pennsylvania. After studying industrial engineering at Lehigh, he became a stockbroker and later, after failing to make his sales draw, left with a colleague to start his own brokerage firm. In 1953, he raised $300,000 from clients and friends and launched the company that later became Safeguard. Its mission was to invest in small start-up companies, funding their growth and then selling off their stakes through public offerings or other placements. He was, in effect, one of the first venture capitalists in the country.

Musser had a special talent for spotting future business stars. He sold Ralph Roberts his first cable system, which later grew into Comcast—the nation's biggest cable company. He encouraged Franklin Mint founder Joe Segal to launch a home-shopping network, which became QVC. Musser was instrumental in launching Novell, the giant software firm.

For most of his life, he lived frugally. He accumulated his wealth gradually, building up a fortune of about $70 million by 1995. He loved his daily routine, which he still follows to this day—rising at dawn, heading to the nearby Radnor Hotel at 6:30 A.M. and eating his granola. He plays tennis at least four times a week, usually at the nearby Aronimink Club. He always has his golden retriever at his side, even in the office.

Musser drove the same Oldsmobile 442, with black-and-white racing stripes, for more than 10 years. He replaced it only after his managers told him no one else at the company felt they could buy a new car while the boss still had his junker. He and his first wife and three kids rarely traveled, except for an occasional weekend at the Jersey Shore or their small house in the Poconos.

"I like my routine of exercise, work, the golden retriever," Pete says. "I prefer that to traveling to some strange city and being a tourist."

Pete gave generously to the community. Whenever the Boy Scouts, local Red Cross or United Way were short of funds, Pete would come to the rescue. He gave to Jewish schools even though he wasn't Jewish, and he gave to Catholic schools even though he wasn't Catholic. Penn State named an auditorium after him and Temple University created an annual "Musser Excellence in Leadership Award."

In the mid-1990s, Pete started developing a taste for dot-com companies. He wasn't a big technology user and to this day he doesn't own a computer and "wouldn't even know how to turn it on." He recently bought a cell phone, which he leaves in his car "so I can remember where it is."

Yet Musser knew the Internet was going to be big business. Safeguard started funding dozens of tech start-ups, like Sanchez Computer and U.S. Interactive and Cambridge

Technology Partners, which quickly became darlings of the stock market.

Around the same time, Musser's marriage started coming apart. In 1992, Musser was at a party at the Franklin Institute and he spotted Hilary, a slender, 27-year-old brunette with hazel eyes, a winning smile and sharp business instincts. She worked in fund-raising for Franklin and Musser walked over and introduced himself. Musser was a major benefactor for the Institute and Hilary knew instantly who he was.

The two became friends and two years later, after his divorce, they started dating. Musser wasn't shy about telling Hilary his net worth.

"I think I used the number $70 million when we met," Musser recalls.

They moved in together in 1995 and bought Bonfield a year later for $2 million, spending another $5 million or more on furniture and renovations.

Musser's lifestyle started becoming more lavish, to the surprise of many of his old friends and business colleagues. He and Hilary spent $4 million for a four-acre piece of property on the ocean in Nantucket. They bought a vacation house in the Poconos, near Musser's old house. They also started their own construction company to start building spec homes in Nantucket.

Hilary, who had a flair for interior design, bought entire showrooms of antiques in France and England. She had a team of artists paint intricate murals around the house, including a China landscape in the dining room. She filled one of their guest cottages in Nantucket with 19th-century enamelware.

"There's no question I changed my living standards

after Hilary, because everybody knows I was more simple, and you can't argue with that," Pete says. "But there was a good side to it, that I got to enjoy beautiful homes and a beautiful living."

For Christmas, the couple usually flew to the Four Seasons in Nevis. Pete threw a special party for Hilary's 35th birthday, inviting more than 100 people to Nantucket for a lobster bake. They built a giant dance floor on the lawn and had it painted with a mural depicting Hilary as a mermaid being chased by Pete, a smiling shark.

On Nantucket, they became close friends with Dennis Kozlowski, the Tyco CEO, and his wife, Karen. That friendship gave them a cameo role in one of the most famous party videos of all time—a film, shown at Kozlowski's trial, of the 2001 birthday party that Dennis threw for Karen in Sardinia in 2001, which featured scantily clad models in Roman attire and an ice sculpture of Michelangelo's *David,* spouting vodka from his penis.

To shuttle back and forth from Nantucket, the Mussers bought a jet. Safeguard had an old King Air that Pete sometimes used for business trips. But in late 1999, he and Hilary decided to upgrade to a used Challenger, which they bought from Home Depot founder Ken Langone. They were able to get the multimillion-dollar purchase fully financed, so Pete could keep all his money in stocks.

"One of the first bills we got for the jet was for a broken windshield, which cost $60,000 to fix," Pete says. "It was outrageous. I was used to the King Air."

Hilary also upgraded his wardrobe.

"When I met Pete he wore pants hiked above his ankles, and he would wear these old short-sleeve shirts and white woven belts. He had no really nice clothes," she says. "So I took him to Neiman Marcus and we bought him a wardrobe, some shirts, pants, a couple of cashmere jackets. People commented that he looked really nice."

She couldn't change his passion for yellow sweater vests. "Pete would never let go of his yellow sweater vests. But I got him to wear better quality. At least now his vests are cashmere cable-knits."

Hilary also tried to get Pete to change his increasingly risky investments—with less success. By the late 1990s, Safeguard was investing in dozens of tech start-ups that had "rights offerings," allowing Safeguard shareholders to buy shares at a discount before the companies went public. One of the early rights offerings was in 1998 for Internet Capital Group, which Safeguard helped launch with a $15 million investment. After ICG went public, Safeguard's investment was worth more than $2 billion. Musser and others who bought the rights offering also reaped huge rewards.

"After that, I was hooked," he said.

He borrowed money against his Safeguard stock, known as "borrowing on margin," and bought more rights offerings. The borrowings meant he was twice as vulnerable to a tech-market downturn, since Safeguard and his tech stocks would both tank at the same time. By early 2000, his margin debt grew to more than $100 million—all of it borrowed against his Safeguard stock.

In late 1999, Hilary started pleading with him to sell some of his Internet stocks or Safeguard holdings. He refused, saying he wanted to keep all his money "in play." Hilary had also amassed a personal portfolio worth more than $100 million—most of it Internet stocks—and she asked if she could sell $20 million in stocks and put the money away for safekeeping.

"I kept saying 'let's just put some money under the mattress' but he never listened to me," Hilary says.

Pete eventually let Hilary collar her stocks, but by then it was too late. The market tanked in early 2000 and their stocks crashed along with it. He refused to sell during the downturn, fearing that his selling would create further declines in the shares of companies he helped create.

Pete says he knew the market was vulnerable to a correction. What he didn't expect was a crash. He also admits he was blinded by his optimism.

"I worried about it, I guess. But obviously I didn't worry enough."

His brokers started calling and demanding their loans back. Since he had borrowed against his plunging Safeguard stock, he didn't have the money. In the fall of 2000, he sat Hilary down on their couch in Nantucket.

"He said, 'Honey, we have a problem. The margin calls are coming faster than I can meet them,'" Hilary recalls. "I knew it was serious. Pete was always quick to tell me when things were good and slow to tell me when things were bad."

Eventually Safeguard agreed to lend him $26 million to pay his margin loans. The move helped Pete keep his Safeguard stock and pay back his loans. But it came at a price. In February of 2000, three directors—all his closest friends—walked into Musser's office and told him to resign.

Pete and Hilary returned the jet. They unloaded some of their Nantucket property, along with the Poconos house and the horse farm. Hilary cut the house staff and started combing over every utility bill, insurance plan and daily expense for possible savings.

One morning, Pete and Hilary sat in the Safeguard lawyer's office and handed over every stock certificate and asset that Pete owned. Hilary kept their properties, since they were in her name.

"That was the bottom, the worst moment," Hilary recalls. "I felt horrible, watching him sign over everything he owned."

Pete stopped going to the country club. Once known for his ceaseless energy and sunny disposition, Musser suddenly looked tired and worn. Some businesspeople started whispering that Musser might get accused of more serious charges, like the other free-spending CEOs of Enron, WorldCom and Adelphia.

"People started treating me differently," he says. "They wondered what else was there, if I was involved in something more serious."

In November of 2000, amid growing financial pressures, he and Hilary married in a small ceremony at Bonfield. Some speculated that they married for financial reasons, so Pete could more easily transfer assets. But they deny that finances had anything to do with the timing.

In 2001, Pete defaulted on his $26 million loan to Safeguard. He negotiated a payment plan with Safeguard and started trying to put his life back together. In 2004, he and Hilary divorced for what they say are "personal reasons."

Today, Pete hasn't given up his dream of leaving this world with a huge fortune. Using his Safeguard connections and nose for new opportunities, he's helped launch or overhaul several companies that he hopes will yield big windfalls. One of them is diet-food seller Nutri/System

Inc., whose stock has gone up more than a hundredfold since the new management took over. Because Musser still owes $15 million to Safeguard, he invested in Nutri/System through his nonprofit foundation, which has about $20 million in assets and is protected from the creditors. He says he hopes someday to get his fortune back to at least $50 million.

"A friend of mine told me I'd make that back in five years," he says. "But that was six years ago."

Hilary is also trying to move on. She bought a home in Palm Beach and still owns the place in Nantucket. She's raising her son, running an interior-design business and becoming an active philanthropist and socialite. When asked what she misses from her old life, she says:

"Not much, really. The jet was the hardest thing to give up. I still really miss it."

On a summer morning in 2006, Pete was giving a brief tour of Bonfield and pointed out a shimmering pond surrounded by flowers and lush reeds. The pond used to be home to two trumpeter swans, Bertie and Gertie. Hilary and Pete adored the birds and bought them a miniature Victorian house to live in.

Today, the little house is empty and the swans are gone. Pete says the birds were eaten by a fox.

"They were terrific swans," he sighs. "They sure had a happy life in that little pond."

6

BARBARIANS IN THE BALLROOM

New Money vs. Old

On a warm, breezy night in Palm Beach, the Grand Ballroom of the Mar-a-Lago Club is ablaze in lights.

Crystal chandeliers sparkle from the ceiling, and spotlights bathe the glittering tables in an orange glow. Gold carvings adorn the walls, ceilings and pillars, along with rows of floor-to-ceiling mirrors. On the main stage, the Michael Rose Orchestra—billed as "South Florida's most popular big band"—kicks off the first few bars of "String of Pearls."

Clusters of white roses hang from the ceiling, and orchids sprout from table centerpieces. When the dinner chimes sound, hundreds of guests stream down a red carpet to mark the start of the annual International Red Cross Ball.

There are tanned trophy wives in skintight Scassi and Isaac Mizrahi gowns. There are nipped-and-tucked social-ites with hair the shape of cotton candy and jewels the size of strawberries. There are real-estate honchos, soft-ware magnates, buyout artists and money managers, all decked out in white ties, tuxes and tails.

A Miami developer chats with a private banker about offshore tax havens. The ambassador from Granada touts his country's tourist potential to a resort developer. "It's the hidden gem of the Caribbean," he says. "This is a ground-floor opportunity."

Jackie Bradley, a buxom blonde squeezed into a jewel-encrusted Joy Cherry gown, chats with friends about her new book, *The Bombshell Bible.*

"It's really more about my inner life," she says. "I'm hoping to use it to help other women like me."

There are tiaras everywhere. Since the Red Cross Ball is the last in Palm Beach to keep tiaras in its dress code, the crown-crazed society queens take full advantage. There are 19th-century tiaras from Britain and borrowed tiaras from Van Cleef & Arpels. Herme de Wyman Miro, the Austrian socialite, sports a seven-diamond tiara given to her by a Prussian countess.

Donald Trump, Mar-a-Lago's proud owner, poses for pictures and greets all the guests. His wife, Melania, the ball's "ambassador of goodwill," offers air kisses to guests while the Donald dispenses with his duties as grand chairman for ambassadorial events. Trump looks proudly out over the ballroom, which, with its confectionary-white pillars and frosted molding, resembles a giant wedding cake.

"You like it?" he asks me, not waiting for an answer.

"We modeled it after the Versailles. You know, Louis the Fourteenth."

With a blaring, trumpet fanfare, a troop of U.S. Marines march down the red carpet with the group of 12 ambassadors. The lights dim, the music stops and the audience prepares for the arrival of the real star of the night.

"Welcome," says a tall and silver-haired man in white tie and tails. "My name is Simon Fireman and I want to thank you all for coming tonight."

After a short speech, Fireman makes his way through the crowd and is surrounded by well-wishers. When he passes our table, an older woman with a white coif and silver tiara sitting to my right leans over and whispers, "This ball used to have class. I bet you money, Fireman will make a fool of himself tonight."

And sure enough, he does.

Blue Blood, Red Crosses

For a half century, the Red Cross Ball has been the premier social event in Palm Beach—an island built expressly for the twin pursuits of wealth and parties. Each year, on the last Saturday in January, hundreds of the island's richest and most celebrated socialites gather for a night of drinking, dancing and donating to the Red Cross cause.

The ball is steeped in Palm Beach history, having been launched in 1957 by Marjorie Merriweather Post, the cereal heiress and high priestess of Old Palm Beach society. Ever since, it has reigned supreme over the hundreds of charity events held every winter on the island. It's the only ball that maintains a dress code of white tie and tiara, and it's the only one that sports traditions like the phalanx of ambassadors and troops of marines.

For decades, nothing symbolized Palm Beach's blue-blood culture like the Red Cross Ball. After Post passed on, the Red Cross torch was passed from one society queen to another, all of whom made sure that only the "right" people in Palm Beach were invited. During the 1970s and 1980s, Listerine heiress Sue Whittmore took charge, making sure that the list was dominated by Huttons, Du Ponts, Hearsts and Whitneys (although occasional exceptions were made for "ethnic" types like Jacqueline Kennedy or Estee Lauder).

The job of the Red Cross chairman was considered the highest social honor in Palm Beach, where society dames from Chicago, New York, Boston and Philadelphia had been spending their winters since the early 1900s. The ball "chairmen" were always women, and always heirs to prominent families. And in Palm Beach's highly matriarchal culture, aspiring socialites worked their way up a complicated ladder of lunches, balls, clubs and dinners in hopes of one day chairing their own ball. The grandest prize of them all was the Red Cross.

"You didn't just show up and become chairman," says one of Palm Beach's old-guard socialites. "You worked at it for a long time to earn the credentials."

This proud tradition helped explain why, in 2005, the Red Cross Ball suddenly became the center of one of the most heated battles ever to hit Palm Beach society.

The man who started it all was Simon Fireman, a hard-driving Bostonian who made his millions from inflatable pool toys. Born to Russian immigrants in the blue-collar Boston neighborhood of Dorchester, Fireman has a penchant for chunky jewelry, brightly colored ties and personal press releases.

After making a name for himself in the Northeast, Fireman moved to Palm Beach via Boca Raton in 2003 and set out to scale the heights of local society. He bought a sprawling mansion on the ocean for more than $6 million. He acquired a local restaurant and spent more than $1 million to turn it into a posh Chinese lounge and local hangout, called CoCo's. He joined Mar-a-Lago and became a fixture on the patio, with a cold scotch and his scrappy assistant, Sumner Kaye (nicknamed "Mini-Simon"), always at his side.

A tall man, with a mane of white hair, a Boston twang and beach tan, Fireman has never been shy about extolling his virtues. In 2005, he commissioned a special issue of *Palm Beach Society* magazine devoted to his life and achievement. The cover headline read: "Simon Fireman: Innovator, Leader, Humanitarian."

He is more reticent when it comes to talking about his legal past. In 1996 federal investigators found that he had funneled $20,000 to the presidential campaign of Bob Dole by making donations through Aqua-Leisure employees. The investigation also revealed he had improperly channeled money to the 1992 Bush-Quayle campaign and other politicians. Fireman pled guilty, and he and his firm paid $6 million in fines. He spent six months under house arrest.

Fireman maintains he didn't know about the contributions, which he said were handled by an underling, and that he pled guilty to avoid a drawn-out legal battle. He later wrote a book arguing that he was an innocent victim of political attacks.

When he got to Palm Beach, Fireman sought to rebuild his image, using charity as the main tool. He donated to arts groups, local hospitals and most of the major balls. At charity events, he became known for grabbing the microphone at the end of the night and announcing pledges of $20,000 or more. While charitable donations have always been the main currency for acquiring social status in Palm Beach, Fireman's flamboyancy and self-promotion went a step too far for the Old Guard.

"Simon Fireman gives to benefit Simon Fireman," says one leading socialite.

Fireman insists he gives from the heart. Over lunch at Mar-a-Lago one afternoon, he told me that giving to others is his greatest joy. To prove it, he pulled from his jacket pocket a two-page spreadsheet of all his charitable donations for over a decade, which he said I was free to publish.

"I can't help myself," he said. "When I see pain and trouble in the world, I have to give. This power overcomes me."

In 2003, Fireman's concern for the world's troubled also helped him score his greatest social coup. He pledged $1 million to the Red Cross Ball, its largest gift ever. The Red Cross abruptly fired the ball's popular chair, Diana Ecclestone, and made Fireman chairman.

Palm Beach society was outraged. They accused Fireman of being a showy arriviste trying to buy his way into society. They also blamed the Red Cross for rudely firing Ecclestone. Several top socialites and donors boycotted the ball, opting to go to a competing ball the same night for battered children. Other donors scaled back their donations.

"Mr. Fireman's behavior isn't what most people in Palm Beach are willing to tolerate," Ecclestone told me.

Fireman shot back that the Old Guard was just trying to keep out new blood.

"People here are worried that they have to deal with a powerful force. Palm Beach can be a closed society. You're not allowed into certain inner circles."

Still, Fireman ignored the critics and remade the ball in his image. He moved it from its longtime home at the historic Breakers hotel to Trump's more bling-friendly Mar-a-Lago. He spent lavishly, paying $700,000 for food, decorations and entertainment, including $200,000 to bring in crooner Neil Sedaka. Because of the big bills, the Red Cross took in only $1.7 million from the 2005 ball— less than Fireman's stated goal of $2 million.

Since so few Palm Beachers attended, Fireman wound up filling the tables with friends from Boston, Washington and Boca. Palm Beachers started referring to the event as the "Fireman Friends and Family Ball."

But the final straw came during his keynote speech during the 2005 ball. Striding up to the podium, Fireman boasted that he had raised more money, landed more ambassadors and thrown a better ball than Ecclestone.

"We have 16 ambassadors this year; last year they had six," he said. "We raised $2 million, last year they raised $1 million."

The speech was a stunning breach of Palm Beach decorum, which held that chairmen never spoke ill of other chairmen, let alone boast about their own successes. Ecclestone and others were furious. They said Fireman hadn't raised as much money as he claimed, since most of it came out of his own pocket. As for the ambassadors, Ecclestone said the important consideration was "quality not quantity." Her Red Cross Ball ambassadors, she said, hailed mainly from European countries, while his included "Syria and Guyana."

"Just because you give a lot of money," Ecclestone said, "doesn't mean you can stand up and make a jerk of yourself."

The Fall from Grace

At the 2006 ball, however, Palm Beach society got its last laugh. The ball started quietly enough. Most of the attendees were doctors, lawyers or accountants from Boston or southern Florida, and they looked noticeably uncomfortable in formal dress, with sagging bow ties and overly puffy dresses. One longtime Palm Beacher said to me: "Last year, there were people here from Boca, and that was bad enough. But this year it's Del Rey. Can you believe it? Del Rey?"

The ambassadors were equally confused, wandering around like lost dignitaries. Granada left early to party at the local bars until 2 A.M. and Lithuania and Liechtenstein stayed at their tables most of the night. The guests munched quietly on their veal chops, cubed sweet potatoes, root vegetables and butter patties shaped like crosses. Frankie Avalon sang "Beach Blanket Bingo" and other 1950s hits. In the year of Hurricane Katrina, the Red Cross touted its good works by honoring Petra Nemcova, the Czech swimsuit model who weathered the Asian tsunami.

"If it was Asia yesterday, tomorrow we might need your help somewhere else," she said, smiling in her Badgley Mischka gown. "Thank you for helping others and spreading the love."

Just when the guests thought the ball would end without incident, Firestone's assistant, Sumner, stood up and made a rousing speech in praise of his boss.

"Simon Fireman is a wonderful human being, a great benefactor and a great leader," Kaye said to the crowd. "His gift of $1 million is the largest ever given to a Red Cross ball. . . . Mr. Fireman is the prime leader. He delivers. I am so proud of our leadership."

The crowd offered muted applause.

As everyone was packing up their jeweled clutches and gift bags to leave, Fireman started making his way to the stage, clearly tipsy after a night of celebrating and honorariums. As he started up the steps, he lost his footing, careened off the stage and fell face-first onto the marble floor.

The supermodel screamed. The marines charged to the rescue. This being the Red Cross Ball, several first responders dashed to the scene and started administering first aid. Fireman lay on the floor, conscious but bleeding. The marines lifted him up and carried him out like a wounded soldier to an ambulance, which whisked him to the hospital. He was treated that night for two black eyes and multiple fractures in his nose.

Fireman quickly recovered and was back on the same stage a few weeks later hosting another ball. But the Old Guard was delighted. Simon Fireman, the brash arriviste who spent millions to reach the top of Palm Beach society and be like them, had literally fallen on his face.

New Money and No Money

The tensions between Old Money and New Money have been around long before the Third Wave. In ancient Greece, the landed wealthy repeatedly feuded with New Money, who were traders making their fortunes from importing and exporting luxury goods like spices, perfumes and linens. Chester Starr, the Greek historian, wrote that the Greek nouveaux, at the same time they were trying to vanquish the Old Guard, were also desperate to be accepted in their social circles. He writes, ". . . the kakoi (nouveaux) who gained wealth and standing sought to imitate the aristocrats socially, and this social assertiveness was probably their most irritating characteristic in noble eyes, even if it was a compliment."

Aristotle, who condemned all wealth as "insolent and arrogant," had especially harsh words for the newly wealthy: "There is a difference between the character of the newly rich and of those whose wealth is of long standing, because the former have the vices of wealth in a greater degree and more; for, so to say, they have not been educated to the use of wealth. Their unjust acts are not due to malice, but partly to insolence, partly to lack of self control, which tends to make them commit assault and battery and adultery."

The battle between Old Money and New Money was especially fierce during the late 1800s and early 1900s, when the industrial and railroad fortunes of the New World started challenging the landed aristocracy of Europe. In Anthony Trollope's famous *The Way We Live*

Now, a fraudulent French financier, Augustus Melmotte, tries to claw his way up the ranks of British society by throwing a lavish party for the Chinese emperor and buying his way into Parliament. The cash-starved gentry covet Melmotte's money but disdain his lack of breeding and naked ambition.

"I dislike those who seek their society simply because they have the reputation of being rich," says Roger Carbury, a proud aristocrat. "I look at him as dirt in the gutter."

The American titans of the Gilded Age, who also had more cash than social graces, were constantly seeking the acceptance and admiration of the European royals. Cornelius "Commodore" Vanderbilt, the uncouth ferry captain, was rarely invited to parties because of his penchant for spitting and pinching the serving girls. John Jacob Astor, who started out trading beaver pelts for a living, famously wiped his hands on his hostess's dress at one social event. Yet New Money can quickly be cleansed of its dirty origins: Ms. Astor become New York's reigning society queen, with her famous "400" list of acceptable New York party invitees.

Today, Richistanis are also crashing the gates of high society and sparking a renewed battle between Old and New Money. Like their Gilded Age forebears more than a century ago, Richistanis are pouring into the nation's wealthy communities and creating a new social hierarchy built on money and more money, rather than breeding and lineage.

They're building giant homes to eclipse the old estates in Palm Springs, Martha's Vineyard, Palm Beach and Greenwich, Connecticut. They're lining up to join the historic golf clubs, yacht clubs, polo clubs and lunch clubs, and when they can't get in (and they usually can't) they're starting clubs of their own.

They're making a run for charity boards, art museums, city opera companies and local environmental groups. They're buying the naming rights to all sorts of public institutions, from hospitals and parks to stadiums and libraries. In 2005, New York financier Ronald O. Perelman bought the naming rights to the main stage at Carnegie Hall, now called the Ronald O. Perelman Family Stage. That followed four other "naming" deals at Carnegie, including the Judy and Arthur Zankel Hall and the Joan and Sanford I. Weill Recital Hall.

For Richistanis, getting into the *Social Register* is passé, not to mention impossible. So they're elbowing their way into a new crop of vanity magazines like *Hamptons, Aspen Peak* and *Gulfshore Life,* which have better party photos and page after page of new boldface names.

Greenwich, Connecticut—once a quiet, blue-blood bedroom community for Manhattan lawyers and doctors—has become a hedge-fund playground filled with flashy billionaires. Local housing prices have skyrocketed, mainly from hedge-fund buyers. Quiet cafés that used to host the ladies-who-lunch crowd have been overshadowed by designer food palaces like L'Escale, which serves crispy duck with grilled pineapple and has a patio overlooking a new yacht club. The old yacht club, Indian Harbor, is bowing to pressure (and money) to host events like "Bermuda Night" for the local hedge-fund association.

Longtime Greenwichers rose up in arms in 2006 against a gargantuan home proposed by hedge-fund manager Joseph Jacobs. Residents said the 39,000-square-foot home was too big—no small accusation in a town filled with 10,000-square-foot mansions. The house featured 11 bedrooms, 16 bathrooms and a 3,600-square-foot gym complete with squash court, golf simulator, massage room, beauty parlor and indoor pool. Jacobs's home followed the 30,000-square-foot home built by SAC's founder, Steven Cohen, who has his own indoor basketball court, ice rink and personalized Zamboni.

The island of Nantucket, once known for shingled shacks and clam diggers, has become a showplace for megamansions and 200-foot yachts. It's also become the land of dueling country clubs. Shut out of the old clubs, Richistanis decided to create their own. The new Nantucket Golf Club is charging up to $400,000 for memberships. Westmoor, a new social club housed on the old Vanderbilt estate, charges $250,000 for membership and features a spa, squash courts and private theater. Another group of Richistanis have gotten together to build the Great Harbor Yacht Club, which would have slips for 40 boats along the waterfront and a modern clubhouse with a pool and restaurant. It's already sold more than 200 memberships at $200,000 each, and members include Abigail Johnson, the billionaire daughter of the Fidelity Investments founder, and trucking magnate Roger Penske.

The feuds are driven by the surging population of Richistanis and its vast wealth, which has far surpassed its Old Money counterparts. Among the nation's richest 1 percent, inherited wealth accounted for only 9 percent of their combined total net worth in 2001, down from 23 percent in 1989. Only a third of the nation's richest 1 percent have received any inheritance or gift, down from more than half in 1989.

As a private banker in Palm Beach explained to me: "If you were a Du Pont in Palm Beach with $7 million a few years ago, you were doing pretty well. You had a mansion, you had nice cars, you went to the charity balls, you had power. Now, with $7 million, you're probably the poorest guy on the block and the guy next to you is building a house three times as big. Life isn't so fun anymore."

The battle is also cultural. The old ruling elite, dominated by the Protestant establishment, Ivy League schools, the *Social Register*, Main Line Philadelphia, Boston Brahmins and New York bankers and law firms, has been crumbling for more than 40 years. E. Digby Baltzell, who coined the term "WASP," predicted rightly in *The Protestant Establishment* that the ruling elite became too insulated from the outside world to remain competitive in a fast-changing economy.

Today, Instapreneurs come from all walks of life, and there is no identifiable "ruling class" or single set of values among the newly wealthy. While Old Wealth prided itself on modesty, tradition, public service, charity and sophisticated leisure, Richistanis pride themselves on their middle-class ethic, self-made fortunes and big spending.

Yet the two also need each other. As the author and heir Nelson Aldrich said to me: "If you're New Money, you have this dream that one day the David Rockefeller of your town will spin through the Rolodex and find your name. And he'll call you up and say 'I need some money from you.' And you'll give him some, and now you're in."

Nowhere are the tensions and attractions more dramatic than in Palm Beach, the tropical sandbox for the superrich since the early 1900s.

Beach Blanket Billionaires

Ever since Henry Morrison Flagler, the Standard Oil baron, turned a patch of Florida swamp into an island paradise, Palm Beach has been the winter playground for the nation's elite. The four-square-mile island has one of the nation's highest concentrations of wealth, at least between Christmas and Easter, when the population swells from 10,000 to over 40,000.

It's also known for its high concentration of scandal, starting from when Flagler left his mentally ill wife, Ida Alice, to marry a 24-year-old, to Marjorie Merriweather Post's divorce from E. F. Hutton after finding him cavorting with a chambermaid in their bedroom at Mar-a-Lago. The X-rated antics of the Pulitzers and the rape trial of William Kennedy Smith (he was acquitted) proved that even through the 1980s, Palm Beach's sex scandals, like the last names, hadn't changed.

Richistanis, however, are radically remaking Palm Beach. The new Palm Beach is younger, richer and harder working. Among the new boldface names on the island is Howard Kessler, a credit-card magnate from Boston, and his wife, Michele, who bought a $30 million home in 1999. In 2006, the Kesslers hosted the Cancer Ball and made it the island's top social event. Sydell Miller, the Cleveland hairstylist who founded Matrix Hair Essentials, built a 30,000-square-foot mansion on the island and has also become a leading benefactor (though the Old Guard still calls her "the shampoo lady"). Palm Beach's other new notables include concert promoter Jon Stoll and his socialite wife, Lori; telecom entrepreneur Dan Borislow; and Dick Robinson, who founded a radio-broadcasting school.

Palm Beach's narrow streets are now jammed with Bentley GTs, Rolls-Royce Phantoms and Porsche Cayennes. Worth Avenue, the main retail strip, used to be a homey collection of upscale mom-and-pops selling French linens, antiques and jewelry. Now it's an onslaught of luxury brands and stark windows that display a single $3,000 Gucci bag or $500 Hermès scarf.

Investor Henry Kravis paid $50 million for a house on the Intracoastal Waterway—a record price for a non-oceanfront property in Florida, brokers say. That was topped in 2005 when construction magnate Dwight Schar bought Ron Perelman's estate in two deals totaling $90 million, making it the most expensive private-home sale ever in the United States.

Donald Trump, not to be outdone, in 2006 listed a home on the island for $125 million. The 60,000-square-foot estate, called Maison de l'Amitié, was owned by health-care magnate Abe Gossman, who went bankrupt. Richistanis in Palm Beach have started buying two or three adjacent properties and putting them together to build bigger and bigger homes. Over the past 20 years, the number of single-family homes in Palm Beach has shrunk to 2,596 in 2000 from 3,008 in 1980, due in part to land mergers and larger estates. Koch Industries heir David Koch bought up three lots to build his 60,000-square-foot mansion, which has one of the largest wine cellars in the country.

Old Palm Beachers used to arrive for the "season"—the four-month period between Christmas and Easter—and rarely did any work on the island, since most of them were heirs, retirees or vacationers. Now Richistanis stay almost year-round so they can claim residency and take advantage of Florida's low taxes. Most run their businesses from their pool chairs, using laptops, cell phones and an army of assistants.

"I like the lifestyle, but my first priority here is making money," says Borislow, a 40-something telecom entrepreneur who drives around town blasting rap tunes from his convertible Bentley. "People used to come here to retire. I'm still hungry. I still have more to prove."

Palm Beach's most popular dining spot used to be the Petite Marmite—a shabbily elegant café known for its veal cordon bleu and past visits by European royalty. Now, the hot hangout is The Palm Beach Grill, a spruced-up Houston's Restaurant known for its burgers and beer.

The all-powerful country clubs, which divided the island by race and religion, are becoming less and less relevant. The rules may be the same—the Palm Beach Bath & Tennis Club and the Everglades Club still have few if any Jewish members, and the Palm Beach Country Club remains almost exclusively Jewish—yet the New Money prefers Mar-a-Lago, which takes anyone willing to pay the $150,000 membership fee, regardless of religion or last names.

When I went for lunch one day at Bath & Tennis (dubbed "Bed Bath & Beyond" by the nouveaux because of its aging membership), the club was filled with silver-haired preppies in white sweaters, polo shirts and khakis, and the big attraction for the day was a bridge class. The restaurant looked like a high-school cafeteria, with lunch ladies standing behind a buffet table doling out breaded fish fillets and steamed corn.

At the next-door Mar-a-Lago, the lunch crowd looks

more democratic—with families in sweat suits, slicked-back real-estate agents and pizza-franchise kings from Ohio.

Says Trump: "The fact that the other clubs are so restrictive has been great for me. It's one of the main reasons we're so successful."

Granted, some things haven't changed in Palm Beach. The social calendar remains one of the busiest in the world, offering more frivolous events per day than most major cities. During a week in Palm Beach I went to three charity balls, ten cocktail parties, two dinners, a champagne brunch, a polo match and a Moroccan couscous party. (I just missed the annual pet parade.)

And for all the talk about rejecting the Old Guard, the new arrivals seem equally interested in re-creating their world. The nearby town of Wellington has become a horse haven, with two new polo clubs, one owned by Outback Steakhouse founder Tim Gannon, and the other launched by a Texas developer.

Social standing remains hugely important, especially to the ambitious, young second wives who now dominate the party scene. There are now three publications covering Palm Beach society—*Palm Beach Society,* the *Palm Beach Daily News* and *Palm Beach Today*—as publicity and flattering party photos have become powerful tools for social elevation. Palm Beachers wait anxiously every Wednesday and Sunday morning for the society column written by the *Daily News's* Shannon Donnelly, arguably the island's most powerful journalist.

Increasingly, though, Palm Beach is becoming two islands—a quiet, fading family of Old Money heirs and a 24-hour beach party of free-spending upstarts. It is the new world of George Cloutier, and the old world of Frank Butler II.

The Setting Son and the Puff Daddy

Franklin Osgood Butler II is preparing for tea.

It's a late Thursday morning in January and Butler, a dapper, 78-year-old scion of Chicago's Butler family, is scurrying around his ramshackle mansion. He's supposed to host two teas on Monday, one for the French Society of Palm Beach and the other for the National Preservation Association. Yet his house is a mess.

The living room drapes are piled on the floor, the ceiling is covered with water stains, and there's a big hole in the wall where the bay window used to be. Most of the damage is from a recent hurricane. But as I walk through the house it's hard to tell what's being repaired, what's under construction and what's falling down from neglect.

Butler is a cheerful, expertly mannered man who says things like "that was Mother's mother, the countess." He is tall and trim from a lifetime of polo, yachting and swimming, and he wears custom-tailored dress shirts with formal wing collars. His voice has a gentle warble, somewhere between early Katharine Hepburn and late Julia Childs.

Butler's family owned the vast tract of land near Chicago that became Oak Brook, Illinois, and the Butler name is plastered all over the local schools, office buildings, parks and golf and polo clubs. He's vague about his jobs throughout life, but says he once ran the family's aviation business. He's also a staunch Republican who says "welfare is a waste of money."

Butler never married and he's still an avid socialite, even if his social circles remain decidedly old school. On a night when most of the nouveaux were headed to the Imperial Cancer Ball at the Breakers, hosted by the Kesslers, Butler was primping for the Colonial Wars/Dames of America Dinner Dance at the Everglades.

He's reluctant to talk about his family's prominence or wealth, lest he appear immodest. Sitting in the parlor one day, I noticed a copy of the *Social Register* sitting on his coffee table and asked how many listings his family had, knowing they had many.

Butler smiled nervously and quickly hid the book under the table. "I'm so sorry. I usually have it turned around so people's feelings won't be hurt. Well, yes, we're in there, because of my mother's family and my father's family. Anyway, that's not important; so you live in New York then?"

Touring the dining room, Butler points to a row of portraits on the wall—all showing women with similar aquiline features, arched brows and aristocratic chins.

"This is my grandmother, Countess Filiponi, when she built Villa Filiponi here in Palm Beach. This is my great-great aunt and that picture was at the Victoria and Albert Museum. This is mother at age 40. This is my great-great-great-great-great-great-great grandmother in 1735, the Duchess of Ormond, and that portrait was done by Blackburn. That's one of my relatives from the Elizabethan period."

The Butler family fortune, or what's left of it, has become the subject of bitter family feuds. Butler's siblings sued him 20 years ago after his father died, and they sued again a year ago after his mother died. Fighting over inheritances has taken such a toll on Butler that he had a

mural painted on his living room wall that shows an elephant and an alligator attacking a young infant.

"I'm the baby," he says, pointing to the mural. "The
nasty elephant and alligator are my brother and sister."

He's also fighting a new lawsuit from his godson, who
also wants money. Butler's house, a Mediterranean-style
mansion overlooking the Everglades Club, has seen better
days. The plaster is crumbling, roof tiles are cracked and
the railing on the front steps is rusted out. Inside, faded
antiques share table space with bowls of moldy fruit, exposed electrical wires and eccentric knickknacks, like a
solid-gold straw Butler uses for drinking champagne.

The house was chopped in half several years ago to
raise money, and the eastern portion was sold off to a New
Money couple. Today, the two pieces are a monument to the
split personality of Palm Beach: Butler's half, a mottled
relic with an overgrown lawn and worm-eaten wood; the
other a crisp, clean villa with lush gardens and new windows and doors.

One afternoon, Butler and I take a drive around the
island, which turns into a tour of his family's decline. He
shows me one of his father's old homes that was sliced
into three pieces, with the 13,000-square-foot "north wing"
of the house recently sold for several million dollars. The
Butler's land holdings, which once stretched from the
ocean to the middle of the island, have been broken up
into dozens of smaller parcels. We turn to another lot,
which was sold years ago to a carpet salesman.

"This sounds terrible, but it shocked me when we had
to sell it to him. This was a carpet salesman, someone
from West Palm Beach; they didn't play bridge, they didn't
go to the same spots, they didn't know the same people.

They weren't anybody; well, that sounds terrible, but you know what I mean."

I ask Butler what he thinks of the new guard, and he says he welcomes the New Money coming to town and fixing up the old homes. But he adds that he's appalled at the way people dress today in Palm Beach, especially at the Breakers. "I see people there in jeans, it's just awful."

When I ask him what life is like at the Bath & Tennis now that they share a beach with Mar-a-Lago, he says, "It's all gone rather well. Except for the Puff Daddy incident."

The "Puff Daddy incident," as Butler tells it, has become something of a defining moment in Palm Beach. Butler was taking his usual afternoon swim in the Bath & Tennis saltwater pool when he heard a commotion. He turned around and saw a crowd of B&T children gathering on the cabana wing to get a better view of the beach.

"It was Mr. Diddy, or Puffy Daddy, you know, whatever he's called. He was there on the beach with a lady friend and they were having relations right there on the chaise lounge. Some members went over and asked them to please stop, but Mr. Daddy became very upset. He actually complained that we were disturbing him."

Puff Daddy, now known as Diddy (the rapper whose real name is Sean Combs), let loose with what the local press called an "invective-laced rap" at the B&T crowd and later complained to Mar-a-Lago about being harassed. Mar-a-Lago complained to the B&T and asked for an apology. Making matters worse, the woman with Puff Daddy wasn't his fiancée, and his spokeswoman said the man on the beach must have been a Puff impersonator.

Either way, Butler said the event traumatized the young B&T members.

"Just think of those little children that watched," Butler says. "No B&T member should have to go through that."

Mischievous George

It's 2 A.M. at a rowdy, beer-soaked bar called Cucina. The song "I Wanna Sex You Up" blasts from the loudspeakers, and a crowd of 20-something partyers, most wearing next to nothing, dances chest to chest in the sweaty, packed room. In the middle of it all, a stout man in a tuxedo holds a Dewars in one hand and a shapely blonde in the other.

"This is what I love about Palm Beach," says George Cloutier, who gets smothered in kisses from passing female acquaintances.

Cloutier, a 55-year-old entrepreneur from Cambridge, Massachusetts, arrived in Palm Beach just three years ago, and in a short time he's become one of the best-known figures on the social scene. He and his girlfriend, Tiffany, attended about 20 black-tie balls in 2006, and the two appear almost daily in one of the island's society newspapers. Last year he donated about $500,000 to charitable functions in Palm Beach—powerful currency in the quest for social status.

"The papers tell me that I'm A-list," he says. "I don't know for sure, but that's what they tell me."

Cloutier is worth an estimated $50 million to $60 million and made his fortune in small-business consulting, advising mom-and-pop lumberyards, family-owned restaurants, gas-station chains and other small firms on how to better manage their finances. It's not a glamorous business, but as Cloutier says, it pays the bills.

George is a typical entrepreneur—fiercely independent, controlling and impatient. He has little respect for inherited wealth, or "fake entrepreneurs," as he calls them who "start out on third base and think they hit a home run."

"Just because you're part of the lucky sperm club doesn't mean you're an entrepreneur," he says. He's also admittedly self-centered.

"I'm an only child and a Leo," he says. "Bad combination."

Cloutier runs his business from one of his two beach homes in Palm Beach and Nantucket. His Palm Beach mansion, a sprawling, new home with a vaguely Bavarian feel, is perched on the ocean and worth an estimated $12 million to $15 million. Most days, he works from his Jacuzzi or recliner chair overlooking the ocean. For his daily executive meetings, he slips on a tie, sits down at his desk and turns on a digital camera above the TV for videoconferences. His two assistants work in the pool house, with a bank of computers, printers and phones.

Managing his business from home gives Cloutier more time for his real pursuit—socializing. With no kids and no wife (he's twice divorced), Cloutier has become a serial ballgoer, heading out in black tie at least twice a week. He also attends most of the "satellite events," like the preball lunches, preball dinners, postball brunches, and pre- and postball parties for the chairmen.

"We're probably out at least five nights a week," he says. "A major part of life here is the balls. I have three tuxedos that I bought a year ago and they already need replacing. They're getting pretty shiny."

A big part of Cloutier's social appeal is Tiffany, a former nurse with blond hair, a gleaming white smile and a Pamela-Anderson-like physique. She's quickly learned the rules of the road in Palm Beach society, like never wear the same dress to two balls.

"Friends could see you in the paper with the same dress," she says. "It can be tacky."

Another rule: You can wear an "important" bracelet with important earrings, but you should never wear them both along with an important necklace, since that would be overkill.

All of which can get expensive. Cloutier says he spends an estimated $80,000 to $100,000 on gowns, jewels and other ballroom battle gear for Tiffany. In 2003, Cloutier spent $35,000 on a diamond necklace for his previous girlfriend to wear for a ball. When they showed up, they were horrified to see three other women were wearing the same necklace, and his girlfriend ran out of the ball in tears.

"That was pretty much the end of that relationship," he says.

The influx of new socialites has turned charity into a closely watched, competitive sport in Palm Beach. At the old balls, socialites typically invited a few hundred of their closest friends and raised under $100,000. Now, money is paramount. To become chairman of a ball today (and receive all the accompanying philanthropic accolades) you have to get all your rich friends to donate heavily to the event. In return, you have to donate the same amount to their balls. The chain of reciprocal giving allows social climbers to essentially buy social standing on the island through charity. And it's all tax-deductible.

"People keep track," Cloutier says. "So if I give $25,000 to your ball, you have to give $25,000 to my ball. If you only donate $10,000 to my ball, I'll notice. It's about giving to a good cause. But it's also about the money. It's really about the money."

Because of his generous giving over the past two years, Cloutier now has enough financial favors to call that he can chair his own balls. He and Tiffany have been asked to chair eight balls in Palm Beach next year, but he says he probably only has time for two or three. He already hosts an annual "Boogie on Low Beach" party at his beach house in Nantucket to benefit the Dana Farber Cancer Institute. Last year, the event raised $60,000. Like most of Cloutier's parties, the Beach Boogie featured lots of sports stars, young women, live bands and free-flowing alcohol.

"I take pride in my parties," he said. "Ask anyone in Palm Beach and they'll say I have the best parties."

ASIDE from having vastly different views of black-tie balls and Christmas parties, New and Old Money also have different views of spending. While Old Money was known for its outward thrift and inner opulence (one blue-blood family in New York described their interior-design style to me as "grandmother's attic"), Richistanis like to flaunt their wealth. And never before have so many flaunted so much.

SIZE REALLY DOES MATTER

"My Boat Is Bigger Than Your Boat"

Don Weston used to feel special cruising the world in his 100-foot yacht. He would motor down to the Caribbean, dock for a few days in St. Martin and meet up with fellow yachters for a leisurely lunch or dinner. His boat wasn't always the biggest in the harbor, but it was big.

"It's the kind of boat that would have gotten a nice christening when it was launched, with a champagne bottle and a big party and everything," said Weston, a retired Cincinnati businessman.

Yet one morning at the 2004 International Boat Show in Ft. Lauderdale, Weston stood on his upper deck overshadowed by giants.

Next door was the *Corrie Lynn,* a 130-foot cruiser with a

king-sized Jacuzzi, five cabins, retractable plasma TV screens and twin jet skis. Down the dock was the 197-foot *Alfa Four*, with an indoor gym, swimming pool and helicopter pad. The talk of the show was billionaire Paul Allen's latest pleasure craft, named *Octopus*, which stretches over 400 feet and has a basketball court, music studio, glass-bottom living room and submarine. *Octopus* has since been overshadowed by *Rising Sun*, Larry Ellison's floating palace that tops 450 feet and has more than 80 rooms on five stories. Along with the usual gyms and swimming pools, *Rising Sun* has a twin-hulled landing craft to carry a four-wheel-drive Jeep ashore.

"I used to think I had a good-sized boat," Mr. Weston sighed. "Now it's like a dinghy compared to these others."

It's safe to assume that at no other time in American history has a 100-foot boat been referred to as a "dinghy." There are so many Richistanis today, with so much money to spend, that they're creating an entirely new level of consumption. Being a truly conspicuous consumer has never been harder, since there are millions of millionaires competing for the same status symbols, and an even greater number of affluent consumers purchasing luxury goods to try to mimic the elite.

According to one study, the nation's richest half-percent consume at the rate of $650 billion a year—equal to the total household spending in Italy. All that spending is pushing up prices in Richistan. The inflation rate for millionaires soared to 6 percent in 2004, compared to about 3 percent for the broader United States. For those worth $30 million or more, inflation rose even further, to 12 percent.

The high-end shopping spree is being driven partly by peer pressure. Keeping up with the Joneses has become fiercely competitive, since there are so many more rich Joneses. George Cloutier, the partyer from Palm Beach, recently bought his girlfriend a cherry-red Mercedes SLK, which cost around $50,000. He thought it was a nice gift. His friends thought otherwise.

"My friends all made fun of me," he says.

So he traded in the SLK for the larger Mercedes SL, which cost around $110,000. Now, two years later, he's getting social pressure to buy his girlfriend an even more expensive car. "Everyone's talking about Bentleys, like that's the car you gotta have."

The pressures have made it harder, and more expensive, than ever to be a truly conspicuous consumer. In his classic 1899 treatise on wealth, *The Theory of the Leisure Class*, Thorstein Veblen coined the phrase "conspicuous consumption" to explain the excesses of the Gilded Age. Veblen said that the wealthy bought expensive goods as a way to identify themselves as members of the nonworking leisure class. Waste and excess weren't just tolerated by the rich; they were necessary to show rank on the social scale. And in a consumer society, rank was signaled by spending.

"The basis on which good repute in any highly organized industrial community ultimately rests is pecuniary strength; and the means of showing pecuniary strength, and so of gaining or retaining a good name, are leisure and a conspicuous consumption of goods." On the flip side, the "failure to consume in due quantity and quality becomes a mark of inferiority and demerit."

The rich, in short, spend to show that they can. What's changed in Richistan is that there are so many Richistanis, with so much disposable income, the job of "showing pecuniary strength" has become increasingly difficult. Just when a Richistani thinks he's staked his claim to the elite, with that 100-foot boat, or $50,000 Mercedes, along comes a richer Richistani with a 250-foot boat, and a Bentley GT.

Richistanis are also spending to outrun the hordes of Richistani wannabes. The growing ranks of affluent consumers are increasingly trading up to buy goods once reserved for the rich. Luxury companies, to grow sales, are happy to sell cheaper versions of their high-end products to serve this new crowd of aspiring shoppers. Marketers call it "mass luxury" and, oxymoron or not, it's made life miserable for Richistani spenders.

Gucci sunglasses, Louis Vuitton bags and Burberry coats are now ubiquitous. Fractional jet companies now allow people to "fly private" for thousands of dollars, rather than paying $30 million for their own plane. You can rent a Ferrari or Porsche from one of the growing number of auto clubs, and you can charter a megayacht for six figures a week, rather than paying the eight-figure tab for ownership. You can join a destination club for $150,000 and vacation at your own seaside mansion in the Caribbean or ski chalet in Aspen. You can even rent a pricey painting to put on your wall from the new crowd of art-rental shops.

The pressures from both the top and the bottom, from richer Richistanis and the mere affluent, have forced Richistanis to create an entirely new class of hyperluxury goods, well beyond the reach of the affluent hoi polloi. In some cases, they're bidding up prices of existing goods. In others, they're launching entirely new categories of products and services, like space travel and "shadow yachts." Either way, the huge numbers of Richistanis are furiously ratcheting up the price of status, and taking Veblen's notion of conspicuous consumption to new heights.

Here's a sampling of some of the traditional luxury markets that are being redefined by the Richistani quest for status.

Yachts: When the Stripper Pole Comes Standard

Sometime in the next two years, the world will see its first private yacht larger than 500 feet. There might even be two. The first, called *Dubai,* is being built for Sheikh Mohammed Bin Rashid al Maktoum, ruler of Dubai, and measures 525 feet. The second, code-named *Eclipse,* is being built for a Russian oil tycoon and is expected to hit the water in 2009. The Russian owner is keeping the actual length a secret, to ensure that his will be the longest. Yet both boats will shatter the record for world's largest private yacht, held for the last 22 years by the 482-foot *Abdul Aziz,* owned by the Saudi royals.

"These days, size matters," says Jonathan Beckett, president of Nigel Burgess, the yacht brokerage firm.

So do numbers. Orders for new yachts longer than 150 feet have doubled over the past decade, to more than 200 a year. Boat builders have more than 15 miles of yacht under construction—longer than the island of Manhattan.

If you want to order a 200-foot boat today, get in line; the waiting list is about two years long. New boats are selling for about $20 million for a 140-footer, to $75 million for a 250-footer. Used yachts are now selling for as much as or more than new ones, since owners are willing to pay up to have their boats immediately.

Upkeep has become even more astronomical. Boat

experts figure it costs about 10 to 15 percent of the purchase price of a boat to maintain it, which means about $2 million a year for a typical 140-footer. Crew salaries are soaring as so many yacht owners search for stewards and captains.

There are so many boats in the water in the United States that yacht traffic jams are becoming a problem. Owners have to book months in advance to get a top berth in St. Bart's around Christmas. Slots at the Ft. Lauderdale Bahia Mar Marina now rent for $7 per foot during the winter months, up from less than $1 a foot in the mid-1990s. Last winter, so many yachts were waiting to pull into Bahia Mar berths that the marina had to deploy special yacht-traffic cops.

Boat builders haven't seen a boom like this since, well, never. The Roaring Twenties had its share of huge boats, like the 407-foot *Savorona,* built for the family that built the Brooklyn Bridge. The *Savorona,* which is still floating, boasted a floor-heated Turkish bath built from 260 tons of hand-carved marble. Yet never have so *many* megayachts hit the water at once. Some of the newly nautical rich are building entire armadas. Paul Allen uses his six-story *Octopus* as a main boat, but keeps his 300-foot *Tatoosh* and 198-foot *Meduse* on hand as backups, and guest yachts for friends and family.

At the Ft. Lauderdale boat show in 2005, I got a glimpse of the latest innovation in boater bling—the 170-foot Paladin, known as a "shadow boat." A shadow boat is a floating garage that tags along with the main yacht and carries all the extra "toys," like cars and smaller boats. It's a kind of yacht for your megayacht. The Paladin, now owned by a

Saudi, holds four to six cars, several motorcycles, jet skis, a submarine and a helicopter. It's also got a decompression chamber, a walk-in freezer, gym and night-vision cameras.

The company that built the Paladin is about to launch a new model called the City of Vegas, with six state rooms, a helicopter deck and, for those boaters who don't like the open water, a full-sized swimming pool.

Gone are the days when "yachting" meant a bracing trip on the family schooner, with billowing sails, wooden bunks and no indoor plumbing. Upper-class boats, as Paul Fussell wrote in his 1983 book *Class,* used to be defined by their discomfort, and their family history.

"Sail is still far superior to power, partly because you can't do it simply by turning the ignition key and steering—you have to be sort of to the manor born. (Probably the most vulgar vessel you can own is a Chris-Craft, the yachting equivalent of a Mercedes.) The yacht must be quite long, at least 35 feet, and in getting a new one you must trade up, never down. According to one yacht broker, boat status proceeds by five-foot increments. The customers, he says, will 'jump up five feet at a time until they get up to 60 or 70 feet.' And the yacht should aim at the uncomfortable racing style, rather than the dumpy, folksy, family style, which might suggest living on it all the time, thus hinting at privation."

Nowadays, sailboats are fine, as long as they can be power-winched back onto the 300-foot motor yacht, like Paul Allen's. (Sailboats now account for a tiny fraction of total yacht sales.) And instead of trading up in five-foot increments, today's move is up by 50 or 100 feet at a time. The new yacht interiors are designed *expressly* to suggest full-time residences, hinting more at floating mansions than at Fussell's "privation."

They have computer-controlled stabilizers, which anticipate the rocking movements of a boat and offset them with underwater fins or gyroscopes, so you forget you're on the water. High-tech security systems, stereos, theaters and 12-person Jacuzzis have become standard. It's not enough to have a helicopter pad; today you need two (one for guests, one for the owner), as well as an indoor storage area to protect the choppers from the salt air.

Guests aboard the *Annaliesse,* a boat that charters for $800,000 a week, enjoy a complete spa with a Roman bath, plunge pools, steam rooms, and a sauna. H. Wayne Huizenga, the garbage and car-dealership magnate, recently purchased golfer Greg Norman's 228-foot yacht, renamed it *The Floridian* and added a helipad and extra guest suite, but he decided to keep the swim-up bar on the sundeck. The 265-foot *Bart Roberts,* a converted icebreaker with a pirate theme owned by Florida businessman Art Gemino, has bronze cannons, a tank of piranhas and a dance floor complete with a removable "stripper" pole.

No one's quite sure when or how the recent battle of the bulge in yachting really started. The first shot was probably fired by Leslie Wexner, the chairman and chief executive of Limited Brands Inc., which owns Victoria's Secret. In 1997, Wexner built the 315-foot *Limitless.* The ship had 3,000 square feet of teak wood along with a gym. A short time later, Microsoft Corp. cofounder Paul Allen bought the 354-foot *Le Grand Bleu,* which quickly proved too small. Allen commissioned a German shipyard to build *Octopus,* billed as the biggest private yacht in the world, with a 59-foot extra speedboat, a swimming pool, a basketball court and a music studio. Its centerpiece is a private submarine, which can be lowered from a special Dr. Nemo–like docking station on the lower deck (although people who've been on the boat say the submarine has been dogged by technical failures). *Octopus*'s total cost: about $250 million.

Even before *Octopus* hit the water, however, a new competitor was emerging. Larry Ellison, the hypercompetitive Oracle Corp. chief, started building the top-secret LE120 project with the same German shipbuilder that made Allen's boat.

When Ellison started building the LE120, it was slated to be 120 meters, or about 393.5 feet. Yet as word got out that *Octopus* would top 400 feet, the LE120 started expanding. When it finally launched in 2004, it measured 454 feet and cost more than $200 million to build. A profile of Ellison and his boat in *Vanity Fair* insisted that the LE120 *Rising Sun* grew during construction to improve its "elegance and speed." "Billionaire one-upsmanship," the article said, had nothing to do with it.

When he took his first holiday on the boat in early 2005, Ellison told friends it was too big—that he and his wife felt like they were the sole patrons in a giant restaurant. "Well, I do think it's excessive," Ellison said. "It is absolutely excessive. No question about it. But it's amazing what you can get used to."

Such megayachts, however, may be reaching their limit. Many of the new boats are so big they can't fit into conventional marinas and have to tie up at commercial ports. When Paul Allen brings *Octopus* to Florida, he can't park next to the other flashy yachts at the Bahia Mar so he has to go to Port Everglades and dock next to the rusty container ships and oily sky cranes.

"You don't spend $200 million on a boat to sit next to a bunch of oil tankers," yacht broker Beckett says. "It's not very scenic."

Some of the new megayacht owners are discovering they don't need, or even like, all that square footage on a boat. The new yachts are so big and so overengineered that they don't feel like boats anymore. Some Richistanis are finding that they actually miss the experience of boating.

"One owner came to me just after buying a huge boat and wanted to sell it," says Henk de Vries, managing director of Feadship, a Dutch yacht builder. "He said that when he stood on the deck, he felt too far from the water."

Real Estate: Greenwich Cottage with Amenities—Pool, Ice Rink, Zamboni

In the late 19th century, the richest Americans started building homes that aspired to the great châteaus of Europe. They were rambling, neoclassical monuments to aristocracy, carved from stone and brick, and tucked at the end of mile-long driveways hidden from public view. They dotted the shores of eastern Long Island, Connecticut and Rhode Island, as well as the rolling farmland of Pennsylvania's Main Line and great plantations of the South.

The grandest was the Biltmore Estate, the French Renaissance-style estate near Asheville, North Carolina, which, with its 255 rooms over 175,000 square feet, remains the largest private home built in America.

Yet Richistanis are catching up. The number of homes built in 2005 larger than 5,000 square feet soared to 30,000—more than five times the number in 1995. These homes now represent more than 2 percent of the total housing starts, up from one-half of a percent a decade ago. In high-end communities like Greenwich, Palm Beach and Atherton, 10,000 square feet is the new normal.

Billionaire financier Ira Rennert built a 66,395-square-foot home on Long Island. PeopleSoft founder David Duffield planned to build a French Norman–style mega-mansion and other buildings totaling 72,000 square feet near San Francisco, but he had to change the plans because of local opposition. The reason: It was too big. Duffield scaled it down to a modest 10,000 square feet.

Hedge-fund manager Steven Cohen paid $14.8 million for a Tudor-style mansion in Greenwich and spent another $10 million or so to increase the size to more than 30,000 square feet, adding an indoor basketball court, a full-sized swimming pool enclosed in a glass atrium and a 6,734-square-foot ice rink. Even the Zamboni has its own gabled cottage.

A home built by Chuck and Karen Lytle on Lake Washington, near Seattle, has a 70-foot saltwater indoor pool ringed with Egyptian columns, complete with hieroglyphics. A 60,000-square-foot home recently completed in Alpine, New Jersey, has a two-lane bowling alley (à la Biltmore), a darkroom, an art room with steel doors that drop from the ceiling, a 2,000-gallon aquarium, 4,000 feet of closets and enough garage space for 19 vehicles.

At one home I visited in Manhattan, owned by a real-estate developer, the wife had so many dresses and suits in her 400-square-foot walk-in closet that she had it equipped with an elevated conveyor-belt system—the kind used in dry-cleaning factories—to store and retrieve her clothes.

Price increases for megamansions have far outpaced the broader market. On the West Side of Los Angeles, there were more than a dozen homes in 2006 on the market for $30 million or more—up from about two in 2001. In 2004, billionaire Ronald Perelman sold his beach house and adjoining land in Palm Beach for $90 million, the highest price ever paid for a residential home in the United States. Even as the housing market cooled in 2006, demand at the top remained strong. The headlines from a single Sunday in late 2006 featured the Manhattan sales of a $46 million mansion, an $18 million condo and $15 million home.

As of early 2007, there were three vacation homes on the market priced at $100 million or more. The cheapest, for $100 million, is an estate near Lake Tahoe named Tranquility, built by a cofounder of Tommy Hilfiger and boasting a private lake, conservatory, boathouse, stable, gymnasium and garage space for 17 cars. The home's staircase is a replica of the SS *Titanic's*, and the marble flooring in the entryway is patterned after the New York Public Library's. Donald Trump is selling a 68,000-square-foot estate in Palm Beach for $125 million, though it's languished on the market for over a year. The new record breaker in real estate is the 95-acre Starwood Ranch in Aspen, built and owned by Saudi Arabia's Prince Bandar bin Sultan, and on sale for $135 million. The estate has a 56,000-square-foot mansion—bigger than the White House—with 15 bedrooms and an elevator. Bandar says he's selling the place because he doesn't get to the mountains much anymore. Yet he won't be homeless in Aspen: He recently built a 15,000-square-foot guesthouse on the property, along with a replica of a British pub, which a spokesman said Bandar will probably keep.

Jets: Reaching Escape Velocity

In 2006 Eric Roth got an unusual request. The head of International Jet Interiors, a New Jersey–based company that outfits private-jet cabins, got a call from a client who had just purchased a Challenger 604. The client wanted something special. Especially for the toilet.

"He asked if I could make a potty seat from alligator skin," Roth recalls. "I said, 'You bet I can!'"

Roth bought two alligator skins from a dealer in Florida for $8,000 and carefully stitched them into toilet seats and trim for the cabin interior. He also installed a handwoven carpet from Thailand, made from wool and silk, with 14 colors, at $600 a yard. He used rose gold, with a "swirled funnel finish," to make the cabin's doorknobs, seat-belt buckles and other fixtures, and he dyed the leather seats the same pinkish hue to match. The cupboards were stocked with Versace china, Christofle silver and Lalique crystal.

"Now *that* was a nice plane," he says.

For some private-jet owners, the world seems to rest on whether they have the proper wood grain on their cabin finish. One of Roth's customers was a woman who owned a Gulfstream IV and insisted on picking out the exact log that would be used to make her interior moldings.

She flew Roth in her jet to a specialty-wood warehouse in Indiana, where they spent eight hours picking through stacks of lumber. Finally she found the perfect piece—a satiny burr madrona. The trip cost $30,000, not including the wood.

Google founders Sergey Brin and Larry Page were more pragmatic about their choice in private jets. The

30-something multibillionaires, who drive environmentally friendly hybrid cars, bought a Boeing 767 wide-body airliner to fly themselves and their friends around the world. The jet, originally designed to hold 224 passengers, was to be retrofitted for a maximum of 50 people.

When asked why they needed such a huge plane, Larry said they were motivated by practical concerns. The plane, after all, probably cost under $15 million—one-third the price of a much smaller Gulfstream 550.

"We tend to have an engineering approach, to be fact-based," Page told *The Wall Street Journal*. "We looked at this and we just did the economics and we said 'you know it makes a lot of sense.' "

Such pragmatic extravagance didn't seem to apply to the plane's interior. Among other amenities, the Google guys wanted hammocks hung from the ceiling. Sergey and Larry bickered over whether they could both have California king–size beds onboard. And at one point during the renovation, according to the designer, Google CEO Eric Schmidt said, "It's a party airplane."

Still, Brin insisted that the private wide-body is fully in keeping with Google's mission to improve the world.

"Part of the equation for this sort of machinery is to be able to take large numbers of people to places such as Africa," Page told *The Wall Street Journal*. "I think that can only be good for the world."

Sales of private jets are skyrocketing. Purchases of new private jets totaled $13 billion in 2005, up from $3.3 billion in 1995. Jet makers like Gulfstream, Bombardier and Dassault sold 750 planes in 2005, more than twice as many as in 1995.

Prices are also rising with demand. The most expensive Gulfstream in 1995 was the $27 million G4. Now it's the $47 million G550. Gulfstream's "entry-level" jet, the G150, now goes for $13 million. But if you want to buy one, get in line. The waiting list for Gulfstreams is now two years long, and some buyers are selling their "slots" on the Gulfstream waiting list for up to $1 million to more impatient buyers. Used Gulfstreams are also becoming scarce.

Airports near the big cities and vacation spots are now swarming with private jets. In Aspen, so many private jets jostle for parking spots during peak times of the year that the overrun has to be diverted to nearby Rifle or Vail. On one day in January of 2006, the airport had to divert 150 planes for lack of space.

Private-jet congestion is so bad at New York's Teterboro Airport that owners have started stowing their planes in Oxford, Connecticut, or Morristown, New Jersey.

"On Friday nights in the summer, Teterboro is like a big parking lot," said Ed Bazinet, a jet owner. "You just sit there, staring at all the other important guys sitting in their jets."

Big-Dog Cars

In the mid-1960s, Rolls-Royce had a problem. Its mammoth Silver Cloud, with its sloping fenders, mantelpiece grille and British pedigree that spoke of empire and aristocracy, had fallen out of favor. Wealth was no longer cool, and the rich no longer wanted to stand out from the counterculture. Especially when it came to their cars.

So Rolls-Royce overhauled its classic design and launched the smaller, more boxy Silver Shadow. It was the proletariat Rolls, more like an embarrassed Volvo than the in-your-face Silver Cloud. Even Rolls-Royce's signature hood ornament, the Spirit of Ecstasy "flying lady," was sent into exile.

Yet Richistanis have ushered in a new era of opulence, and with it, a return to flashy rides. After being acquired by BMW in 1998, Rolls-Royce dusted off the blueprints for the Silver Cloud and in 2003 unveiled the new Phantom— a 2.5-ton, 19.5-foot-long whale of a car with a $320,000 price tag.

"People today are more comfortable standing apart," said Bob Austin, a Rolls spokesman. "Wealthy people have regained a certain confidence. Suddenly if you want to stand out, you need something special. This is a big-dog car."

And the big dogs want to drive themselves. Before 1980s, the "vast majority" of Rolls buyers used chauffeurs, Austin says. Now, about 95 percent of Rolls owners drive the cars themselves, especially since the Phantom's 453-horsepower V-12 engine can power the car from 0 to 60 mph in 5.7 seconds.

"The new breed is younger, and they like to experience things themselves," Austin said. "They don't want to spend $320,000 on a car like the Phantom and let the chauffeur have all the fun."

Not to be outdone, Mercedes has resurrected the Maybach, a famed luxury car made in Germany in the 1920s and 1930s. Measuring more than 20 feet long, the Maybach 62 costs $358,000 and has a top speed of 155 mph. Maybachs aren't sold by salespeople—they're "presented" by "relationship managers." The backseats contain a refrigerator, a retractable champagne holder (with glasses) and extendable leg rests. The seats can be heated or cooled, or set to the "pulse" massage setting.

Bentley, now owned by Volkswagen, returned to the Roaring Twenties to build its latest Continentals, which sell for a more modest $150,000. Bentley says that with so much demand, it doesn't have to do any traditional corporate advertising. Says a spokeswoman: "Those who can afford the cars will find us."

Meanwhile, the classic luxury brands of BMW, Mercedes and Jaguar have lost some of their cachet. Says Austin: "Those cars have become almost . . . well, I hate to say this, but almost common."

Painting by Numbers

In 1981, Barney Ebsworth, a St. Louis travel-agency owner and art collector, gave a short speech at the St. Louis Art Museum. The art market, he said, was headed for a huge run-up in prices. The reason: simple supply and demand.

Ebsworth saw more and more entrepreneurs like him making huge fortunes. And most of them were buying big houses and looking for showpiece art to fill up the walls. Yet the amount of "quality" art available was actually shrinking. Quality, of course, is subjective in the art world. Yet Ebsworth believed that there was little new art being created that would withstand the test of time. And there was a shrinking supply of Picassos, Mirós and de Koonings.

"In my business, I could see this incredible amount of wealth being created and trade barriers coming down," he says. "It was like money and wealth were being manufactured. But some of the things that wealth likes to buy, like art, were not increasing at all. After the 1970s, there was a general falling-off in the quality of American art. There wasn't enough new supply to meet the demand. If you looked at a chart, the demand side was going up at a 47-degree angle. The supply side was going down."

The result: "We were about to see geometric increases in prices."

At the time, art dealers and collectors thought Ebsworth was nuts. Now they wish they had listened. When Ron Lauder in 2006 bought Gustav Klimt's *Adele Bloch-Bauer I* for $135 million—the highest price ever paid for a work of art—the art press was stunned. Ebsworth wondered why it took so long.

"It won't be long before someone buys a piece for $150 million and then $200 million."

Today, Ebsworth is riding the top of the wave. As one of the leading collectors of postwar and contemporary art, Ebsworth has amassed a collection valued at between $200 million and $300 million. He owns Warhol's famous *Campbell's Soup Can with Can Opener,* the only one of Warhol's iconic large paintings that's in private hands. He also owns a prized de Kooning and Edward Hopper's famed *Chop Suey.*

Ebsworth has never sold a significant painting. Yet in recent years his purchase of modern works has slowed, mainly because he refuses to pay more than $10 million for a picture, pricing himself out of the market for big postwar pieces. The most recent piece he purchased was a 17th-century Dutch painting.

"The stuff that's good out there is going for $20 million or $30 million," he says. "I run away from the big-dog syndrome in the auction room, where one big dog is trying to beat out the other big dogs."

It's not the high prices for "quality" art that bother Ebsworth. Picasso's *Boy with Pipe,* which sold for $104 million in 2004, he says, was "worth every dollar." So was the Klimt. What troubles him—and signals an irrational market, fueled by Richistani competition—are the huge prices being paid for bad art.

"When you see a late '60s Picasso selling for more than $15 million, that's crazy. That was his weakest period. These people have a lot more money than smarts. They're buying the name, nothing else. The dealers are flakking these B-minus pictures as if they're great works, and buyers don't know the difference."

The art market hasn't seen such a run-up in prices since the late 1980s. And while many say history is bound to repeat itself—with a speculative bubble followed by a sudden collapse in prices and demand—others say supply and demand will dictate a continued rise in prices. There are, quite simply, too many rich people chasing the same paintings.

The big auctions in New York have become like spectator events for competitive spending. Sotheby's and Christie's racked up combined sales of $729 million during their fall 2006 contemporary-art auctions—more than 10 times their total in 2000.

Richistanis like their art large and loud. As one New York dealer told me, "Today's collectors are buying with their ears, not their eyes." And they want brand names.

They want their guests to notice the Picasso signature above the dining table or the Jackson Pollock splatter painting next to the big-screen TV.

"They've got the yacht and the three homes, so what's left?" Ebsworth says.

Beyond filling space on their walls, the New Rich have been convinced that art is an investment product. Wealth managers, financial advisers, art dealers, galleries and auction houses have all colluded to push the concept of art as a way to make money. A Chuck Close portrait isn't just a painting; it's a "noncorrelated asset." Art doesn't just balance the living room; it balances your portfolio.

By turning art into a financial product, art dealers have made the market much more appealing to Richistanis. Richistanis may not understand the cultural importance of *Campbell's Soup Can with Can Opener,* but they do know that price increases for Warhols have far outpaced the stock market in recent years. The Mei Moses Fine Art Index, which aggregates the prices of artworks that have been sold publicly at least twice over their lifetime, has handily outperformed stocks in the past five years.

No group of Richistanis has transformed the art market more than hedge funders. Young, newly wealthy and eager to break into the ranks of the New York cultural elite, hedge funders have cleverly adapted their trading expertise to the art world.

Kenneth Griffin, the founder of Citadel Investment Group in Chicago, paid more than $60 million in 1999 for Paul Cézanne's *Curtain, Jug and Fruit Bowl.* Steven Cohen has run up an art tab of more than $700 million in recent years, buying a $52 million Jackson Pollock for his library, a Van Gogh and a Gauguin for the living room (purchased for a combined $100 million), and a Warhol and Lichtenstein for his foyer. Cohen paid between $8 million and $12 million for Damien Hirst's pickled tiger shark, which needed a complete makeover after the creature started decomposing.

Many hedge funders have become savvy art flippers, using their expertise in financial trading and market-making to buy and sell paintings. Contemporary art is especially attractive, since prices are set more by trading activity than by history and critics. In 2003, Dan Loeb, the 43-year-old hedge-fund manager partner at Third Point LLC, bought a painting called *UNO-Gebaude Haus per la pax,* by the German artist Martin Kippenberger. In 2005, he sold it to British collector Charles Saatchi for a 500 percent profit, making a quick $1 million.

"With this kind of art, you can make your own taste," quipped hedge-fund manager James Chanos.

Some hedge-fund managers invest heavily in one or two artists, build up a "position" and help boost their prices before unloading the works at a profit.

David Ganek, who manages Level Global Investors, built up a sizable position in the works of photographer Diane Arbus. Mr. Ganek and his wife last year pledged 13 rare Arbus prints to the Metropolitan Museum of Art, including the well-known "A Young Waitress at a Nudist Camp, N.J., 1963," and "A Family on Their Lawn One Sunday in Westchester, N.Y., 1968."

Mr. Ganek also helped promote an Arbus show at the Met, which boosted her profile and prices. At the same time, he quietly sold off one of his Arbus prints for a profit.

"These hedge-fund guys like to trade," says Andrew Fabricant, a major New York dealer and a director of the

Richard Gray Gallery. "For them, the instinct to trade in and out of financial issues or in and out of pictures is equally compelling."

In fact, some of the artworks snatched up by hedge-fund traders have turned out to be better investments than wall hangings. Hedge funders have filled their office walls with their prized works to impress clients and friends. But the works don't always translate in the uptight world of investing. Dan Loeb proudly displayed in his office one of Richard Princes's "Biker Chicks," showing a topless woman on a motorcycle, until his rabbi came to the office and asked him to cover it up.

Chanos hung a pricey Gerhard Richter painting in his office, thinking it would add a touch of sophistication. Instead, an important client mistook it for a child's finger painting. The piece now hangs in Chanos's home.

Watches: If You Have to Ask, You Can't Afford It

In 2006, the New York–based Luxury Institute—a group that researches the wealthiest 10 percent of consumers—did a survey to find out which brand of wristwatch was the most prestigious in the country. To make sure they were getting quality opinions, they polled people with net worths of more than $5 million. The result: Rolex barely made the top 10, Cartier ranked 13th, and the vaunted Breguet brand ranked 5th.

The winner was Franck Muller, a newcomer from Switzerland that sells fewer than 4,500 watches a year in the United States.

"We could easily sell more," says Hratch Kaprielian, president of Franck Muller USA. "But then our watches would become common."

Not likely. Franck Muller is one of a number of new brands known only to the rich. They haven't been commercialized or cheapened by mass marketing, at least not yet. And you can only buy them in small boutique shops (appointments required). Their prices ensure that the club of owners remains small and exclusive.

The cheapest Franck Muller watch, made from quartz and stainless steel, costs $4,800. The most expensive models now sell for more than $600,000.

For its signature piece in 2006, the company produced the Aeternitas, with an eternal calendar with split-seconds chronograph. The watch promises to tell the day, date, months and moon phase for the next 1,000 years (yes, it does take into account leap years). The price: $736,000.

Swiss watch exports in the United States grew 17 percent last year and totaled about $170 million in 2006, up from $136 million in 2004. While Rolex, Cartier, Piaget and Patek Philippe continue to dominate sales among the traditional elite, Franck Muller has become the timepiece of choice for the New Rich.

"It's like a private club," Hratch says. "When you're wearing a Franck Muller and you see someone else wearing one, you *know*," he says, with a wink.

Hratch, a Turkish jeweler who wears gold bracelets, diamond-studded watches and striped T-shirts, manages Franck Muller USA from an old warehouse building in downtown Manhattan. I asked him what makes a watch worth $600,000 and Hratch frowns.

"Our buyers, they would never ask this question. But

I will try to explain it to you. A watch has to be interesting. It has to be complicated. It has to be beautifully designed, and look good. It has to be a watch that you wind every morning, you clean the parts, you admire the craftsmanship. You build a relationship with your watch."

A good watch, he adds, is also a statement. Before Franck Muller came on the scene, luxury brands were competing to make the thinnest watch possible. Franck Muller crashed the market with big, jewel-encrusted designs with oblong faces and artsy designs.

Form follows function with Franck Muller: One of its most popular watches is the Crazy Hours, a $20,000 timepiece that features mixed-up numbers on the face. The number 8 is placed where the 12 should be, and the 2 is where the 6 usually sits. The hour hand jumps five places to get to the correct time, while the minute hand moves normally.

I ask a company spokeswoman if Crazy Hour owners can actually tell the time.

"At first, it's tricky," she says. "People have trouble with the numbers, since they're all over the place. But the concept of the watch is to get people to think about time in a different way. It's to get them to notice that every moment is fleeting. Once they understand that, they have a much easier time with the watch."

Or, as a *BusinessWeek* reviewer recommended, you can wear two watches: the Franck Muller watch to get attention, and the second watch to find out what time it is.

Experiences: If It's Tuesday It Must Be the Maasai Village

Gordon MacGeachy describes himself as a lifestyle-management expert. But his real job, as co-owner of Mint Lifestyle, is arranging new fantasy "experiences" for the rich. For a fee of $20,000 a year, MacGeachy can get you a private tour of the Tower of London, a safari in South Africa followed by a meeting with Nelson Mandela or a front-row seat at NASA's control center during a shuttle launch.

Consider the itinerary he created for a 30-something dot-commer who wanted to "experience" Scotland. The cost of the 10-day trip: $280,000.

> MONDAY AUGUST 7. Champagne on the lawn of a castle, followed by dinner, and a whisky blending-and-tasting session with world-famous whisky expert Ian Buxton and a historian's account of the Battle of Culloden.
>
> TUESDAY AUGUST 8. Depart in helicopter to Highlands, rendezvous with Land Rover for a 4 × 4 driving experience. Wildlife tour with golden eagles and red deer. Rifling will follow. Lunch with champagne, langoustine, beef filets and live squeeze-box music. Falcon display. Board helicopter to river canyon for rafting trip.
>
> WEDNESDAY AUGUST 9. Proceed to Skibo Castle for grouse shooting. Chopper flight over beaches of the north coast of Rom before party at the Three Chimneys resort in the Isle of Skye. Fly to Donegan Castle and transfer to the Carrour Estate— a private castle on 5,000 acres.

For a client who liked space travel, Mint got special access to the Kennedy Space Center in Florida and a seat in a VIP area to watch the space shuttle launch—a privilege unavailable to everyday taxpayers. For the more ambitious space traveler, there is Virgin Galactic, which is already filling up its suborbital flights at $200,000 per ticket.

For a client who liked cars and wanted to visit Germany, Mint arranged a meeting with the directors of BMW, followed by test drives of a secret new car and a "spy's tour" of Berlin with Markus Wolf, the famous cold war spook.

"These are people who have already done all the Aman Resorts and Four Seasons, and they want something special," says MacGeachy. "They want to experience things that the normal person couldn't even imagine."

At the same time, Richistanis want "genuine" experiences. They want to escape their complicated world of private jets, multiple estates, house staffs and entertaining schedules and see how the other half lives. They want the simple life, at least for a day or two. Mint helped one wealthy client take her kids to a rural village in India and dig ditches for two weeks.

Says MacGeachy: "She wanted her kids to know that the world they know isn't the world that most people live in."

Or consider this letter from a multimillionaire Mint client who went to Africa to live among the rural Kenyans, while also mixing with royalty.

"The Maasai village visit was a lifetime experience that I can't even begin to articulate," the letter began. "Also, the expert professor guide, the cooking lessons at the castle and exclusive lunch on the island above Vic Falls were not things normal people thought were realistically possible."

Plutonomics

The status spending by Richistanis has created a new world of consumption at the top. Yet their shopping spree is also sending giant ripples through the American economy.

The first and most obvious effect is trickle-down spending. Or, in the words of John Kenneth Galbraith, "If you feed enough oats to the horse, some will pass through to feed the sparrows." And today's Richistanis are passing a lot of oats.

One day in the summer of 2005, I was in Greenwich, Connecticut, working on an article about wealthy hedge funders. I wanted to find out how they were transforming the town, and one of my stops was Miller Motorcars, the local purveyor of Ferraris and Bentleys. I was chatting with the general manager, Richard Koppelman, when one of his salesmen came over and said he had a buyer for a red Ferrari 360 Spider, priced at $225,000. I figured it had to be a hedge funder.

"What does he do?" Koppelman asked.

The salesman paused. "Well," he said, "he's a stonemason."

I peered into the showroom and sure enough, there was a middle-aged man in work boots, shorts and a T-shirt, covered in concrete and dust. He was standing next to the Ferrari, holding a checkbook. I walked over and asked him how he had become so successful.

"Stone walls," he said. "And patios, and marble, you know. All these new houses need new walls."

The hedge funders were building so many grottoes and stone walls in town that they had made the stonemasons rich—or at least rich enough to buy a $225,000 Ferrari.

The financial columnist Dan Gross calculated that the top 1 percent of earners in New York City may support about 153,000 service jobs. "One hedge fund manager who spends $1 million annually on services—a driver and house staff, investment and real-estate brokers, restaurants and psychotherapists—probably sustains 25 livelihoods."

To get another view of the trickle-down effect, I asked three Richistani families to send me their expenses for 2005. I reproduce them here without their names, since even the proudest Richistanis wouldn't want the world to know they spend $80,000 a year on massages. (None of these families are profiled elsewhere in the book.) Although some of the expenses are onetime items (like cars or yachts), they give you a rough idea of how much today's rich are spending.

ANNUAL EXPENSE STATEMENT NUMBER ONE

$50 million net worth

Mortgages, two homes	$ 400,000
Insurance	$ 70,000
Utilities	$ 24,000
Real estate taxes	$ 200,000
House staff and personal assistants	$ 500,000
Gardening/pools maintenance	$ 140,000
Charities	$ 500,000
Restaurant/bars	$ 60,000
Cars	$ 300,000
Schools	none
Personal beauty/salon/spa	$ 27,000
Clothing	$ 30,000
Air charters	$ 350,000
Club memberships	$ 225,000
Political contributions	$ 61,000

ANNUAL EXPENSE STATEMENT NUMBER TWO

$80 million net worth

Mortgage	$ 64,000
Real estate taxes	$ 32,000
Insurance	$ 31,000
Utilities	$ 31,000
House staff and personal assistants	$ 315,000
Gardening/pools maintenance	$ 146,000
Home furnishing and appliances	$ 93,000
Household supplies	$ 43,500
Charity, political contributions	$ 11,000
Cars	$ 8,500
Schools	$ 34,000
Travel	$ 500,000

ANNUAL EXPENSE STATEMENT NUMBER THREE

$1.2 billion net worth

Mortgages	*none*
Real estate taxes (per year)	$ 900,000
Insurance	$ 500,000
Utilities	$ 700,000
House staff and personal assistants	$ 2,200,000
Annual maintenance of real estate (ex staff listed above)	$ 900,000
Charity, philanthropic events	$ 3,000,000
Restaurant/bars	$ 250,000
Cars...........................	$ 1,000,000
Children's schools	*none*
Personal beauty/salon/spa .... (includes $80,000 for massage)	$ 200,000
Clothing	$ 300,000
Air charters/private jet	$ 3,000,000
Club memberships	$ 500,000
Political contributions	$ 100,000
Yacht(s) (purchased new boat last year) .. ($1,500,000 for salaries alone)	$20,000,000
Entertaining (at house)	$ 2,000,000

All those massages and million-dollar parties and jet rentals may sound like pure indulgence. And "trickle-down" economics has failed to make a dent in America's growing inequality gap. Yet Richistani spending is becoming an increasingly important part of the U.S. economy, if only because Richistanis now control so much more wealth. In 2005, an equity strategist at Citigroup, Ajay Kapur, started wondering why the American economy wasn't slowing more rapidly in 2005 given the sudden increase in oil prices.

Kapur came up with a theory he called "the plutonomy." In plutonomies, like the United States, Canada and the United Kingdom, the wealthy account for a greater share of national wealth, spending, profits and economic growth when compared with other developed countries. Kapur figured that the top 20 percent of income earners account for as much as 70 percent of consumption in the United States. Like it or not, he said, spending by the rich was propping up the economy, even as the middle and lower classes were struggling.

In places where plutonomies exist, Kapur wrote, "There are rich consumers, few in number, but disproportionate in the gigantic slice of income and consumption they take. There are the rest, the 'non-rich,' the multitudinous many, but only accounting for surprisingly small bites of the national pie."

So rather than trying to figure out why the average American consumer was still spending despite rising oil prices, Kapur focused on the wealthy. He found that since the wealthy had so much disposable income, they were largely unconcerned and unaffected by the rise in oil prices. The continued spending by the rich was, in fact, propping up the rest of the consumer economy. As one yacht owner said when I asked him if he worried about rising fuel costs: "So it costs me $60,000 to fill up instead of $40,000. That's nothing for a boat that costs $5 million a year to maintain."

In this new plutonomy, with "rich" consumers and "everyone else," companies that serve the rich are prospering. From department stores to hotels to automakers to home builders, businesses in every industry are adapting to an increasingly hour-glass-shaped economy, selling to the status-seeking rich, and the penny-pinching middle and lower middle classes. There's Wal-Mart or Neiman Marcus; the Four Seasons or La Quinta; Jet Blue or Flexjet.

The companies that succeed in grabbing the Richistani market will likely be among the biggest winners in the coming years, with higher growth rates, fatter profits and better-performing stocks. Pricing power at the top of the consumer chain has grown, even as chains like Wal-Mart and Target cut prices to hang on to their markets. "Pricing in this market is like pushing an open door—there's no resistance," says Natasha Pearl, owner of the Aston Pearl concierge service in New York. "I think some of the new money is worried that it's tacky or rude to negotiate at this level. In general they are less experienced than this type of consumer in the past."

Businesses that have succeeded in Richistan are already outpacing the broader market. As part of his stock research, Kapur created an index from shares of companies that cater to the rich, including Julius Baer, the private banker; Bulgari; Richemont, which oversees Cartier, Dunhill and other brands; Kuoni, the upscale travel agency; and Toll Brothers, the luxury home builder. Since 1985 the Plutonomy Index has increased by 17.8 percent a year, well outperforming broader global indexes.

One way to get richer, in other words, is to invest in companies that serve the rich. With the population of rich people expanding so rapidly, wealthy consumers have gone from being a niche market to a broad consumer base. The old economic adage of "Sell to the classes, live with the masses" no longer holds quite as true, as those who sell to the "classes" are making "classes" money themselves.

Yet while the rich are accounting for more of the nation's spending, they're also accounting for more of the nation's debt. Despite their huge new fortunes, many of today's millionaires—and even billionaires—are living beyond their means. The nation's richest 1 percent took on $383 billion in debt between 1995 and 2004, most of it in the form of mortgages and installment debt. Their debt grew 235 percent between 1989 and 2004, while their total wealth grew at half that rate. The nation's richest 5 percent now acccount for 20 percent of its debt. All those yachts, wine, cars, art, house staff and alligator-skin toilet seats are starting to chip away at the fortunes of Richistanis—especially as their investment returns decline in a slowing stock market. The runaway spending by Richistanis may help explain why, even though their share of America's income is growing, their share of wealth has remained roughly the same since the 1980s. Richistanis, in short, are spending too quickly to accumulate more permanent wealth.

Even the richest of today's rich can face short-term cash crunches. Take the case of Larry Ellison, who was ranked number four on the Forbes list of richest Americans in 2006, with an estimated fortune of $19.5 billion, most in Oracle stock.

In a series of e-mails in 2002, Ellison's financial adviser, Philip Simon, pleaded with Ellison to cut back on his spending because he was reaching his credit limit of more than $1 billion. While Ellison's stock is worth far more, he preferred to borrow against the shares rather than sell them. He was spending $194 million on his yacht, $25 million on a villa in Japan and $20 million a year on "lifestyle."

"I'm worried Larry . . ." Simon wrote in one e-mail. "I think it's imperative we start to budget and plan." He later added, "We have a freight train going down a track, hitting a debt wall."

Some economists see a darker side to the luxury boom. The trickle down in spending has been accompanied by a trickle down in aspirations. With so much wealth parading around, the middle class and even upper middle class suddenly feel poor by comparison and are spending beyond their means to try to keep pace.

In his book *Luxury Fever,* the economist Robert H. Frank writes that lavish spending at the top has set a new standard for middle-class and lower-income families to try to emulate. Since their own wages are flat or falling, everyday consumers are going into debt, working longer hours and spending less time with their families to try to keep up. The flood of high-end products for Richistanis has also set a new, irrational reference point that consumers will use when making their own purchasing decisions. Frank cites a personal example of shopping for a gas grill. His previous grill, which he bought in the 1980s, cost $89.95. When he went looking for a new one, however, he discovered the seven-foot-long, stainless-steel Viking-Frontgate Professional Grill for $5,000.

"The real significance of offerings like the $5,000 Viking-Frontgate Professional Grill, for most of us, is that their presence makes buying a $1,000 unit seem almost frugal. As more people buy these up-market grills, the frame of reference that defines what the rest of us consider an acceptable outdoor grill will inevitably continue to shift. . . . In short both the things we feel we need and the things available for us to buy depend largely—beyond some point, almost entirely—on the things that others choose to buy."

As a result, Frank argues, the nation's nonrich are wasting their time and money trying to keep up with the wealthy. They are also, he says, ruining the environment and their communities in the process. The race to make more money to keep up with the rich, he says, is the reason Americans are spending less time with children and less time sleeping. It's also the reason Americans feel less happy, since happiness is partly determined by how well we're doing compared with those around us. The race, he said, will only get more destructive as the rich get richer and more numerous.

"Chief executives will have to signal their wealth and position by building houses with not 50,000 square feet of living space but 100,000; by buying cars that cost not $100,000 but $200,000; wristwatches that cost not $25,000 but $50,000; and so on.

"These new higher levels of spending will cause continued escalation in the community consumption standards that others feel compelled to meet."

In sum, the Richistani penchant for profligacy has created new benefits and dangers for the economy. It's supporting new service jobs for waiters, butlers, maids and Bentley dealers. But Richistanis are also helping to push the United States deeper into debt, both through their own borrowing, and through the borrowing of everyday consumers trying to mimic their spending.

FOR all their excess, however, Richistanis are also a charitable lot. And just as they are redefining luxury, they're also redefining charity. Their new methods of giving have proven highly controversial. But if they're successful, and if they follow through on their promises to donate large portions of their fortunes (both big *ifs*) , Richistanis could help bring about sweeping changes in everything from health care and science to the arts, global poverty and education.

8

PERFORMANCE PHILANTHROPY

Giving for Results

Philip Berber loves picking fights with the status quo.

A Jewish Irishman who now lives in Texas, Berber has spent most of his 45-year life dreaming up technology companies that disrupt the establishment. In the mid-1990s, he created CyBerCorp, an online trading system that allowed individual investors to buy and sell stocks directly from their home computers. The premise was revolutionary—to bypass brokers like Merrill Lynch and usher in a new era of do-it-yourself (and lose-it-yourself) investing. When the Internet took off, so did CyBerCorp, allowing Berber to sell the business to Charles Schwab Corp. in 2000 for more than $450 million.

"For a Jewish kid from Dublin, that was more money than I ever imagined," he says, in his Southern-fried brogue.

Now, from a makeshift office in suburban Austin, Berber is launching a new venture that could be even more revolutionary.

Dressed in his dot-commer uniform of khakis and polo shirt, Berber dashes around his conference room outlining his business plan. His new company, he explains, is akin to a venture-capital fund, investing in start-ups and entrepreneurs. Like CyBerCorp, it bypasses an entire industry of financial middlemen to deliver services more efficiently. He talks about his returns on investment, his quantitative analyses and rigorous project management. He fills a notepad with dozens of flowcharts, X-Y graphs and maps of his market area. He goes on a tirade about his competitors, who he says are "wasteful" and "arrogant."

"What I'm doing is very akin to the Dell (computer) model," he says. "It's a direct delivery of a product."

The only difference is that Berber's business doesn't make a product. It doesn't have a sales department, or advertising, or growth targets, and it doesn't make any money. His company, in fact, is in the business of *giving away* money. It's called A Glimmer of Hope, and it's Berber's personal charity. So far he's given Glimmer $100 million, or about half his total fortune. And in the process, he's helping to create a new kind of entrepreneurial charity.

Berber insists he's not "giving away" his money. He hates black-tie balls and the social climbing that poses as charity in places like Palm Beach. He shuns awards and would never think of writing a check to a big institution like the Red Cross, which he says wastes donor money on staff, marketing and useless reports.

Instead, Berber calls himself a "social entrepreneur." An impatient man, with a cleanly shaved head, a runner's physique and a lightning-fast mind, Berber has decided to run his charity more like a tech start-up. He's not in the business of donating money; he's in the business of investing in social change, demanding concrete results and searching for dot-com-style efficiencies.

"I'm not giving anything to anybody," he says. "There is no charity with me. I'm a social investor investing capital for social profits."

Berber's plan to save the world through return-on-asset models would be ambitious by any standard. Yet he's taken his experiment one step further. He's decided to apply his social-investor theories to one of the most complex and intractable social problems in the world—poverty in Ethiopia.

So far, Berber is posting impressive results.

Since 2001 Glimmer has spent more than $16 million in Ethiopia. It's built 1,657 water wells, bringing clean water to more than 886,000 people. It's built 190 schools, educating more than 112,000 students. It's created 99 health clinics, serving 766,000 people, and launched 24 vet clinics for farm animals, benefiting 162,000 people.

He's even prouder of his efficiency. Berber's projects in Ethiopia, he says, sometimes cost half as much as similar projects run by the big aid groups. He can deliver water, for instance, for $5.74 per person, or health care for $4.01 per person.

"This isn't rocket science," says Berber, who has actually worked in rocket science. "There is no magic to what we're doing. This is applying fundamental lessons I learned as a business entrepreneur and reapplying it as a social entrepreneur. This is a blueprint and it is wholly applicable to whatever philanthropic cause touches anybody's heart. I only wish more people would try it."

He's already winning converts. Computer billionaire and fellow Texan Michael Dell has donated $500,000 to Glimmer, and Silicon Labs founder Dave Welland has also donated several hundred thousand, even though Berber isn't seeking outside money. In the summer of 2006, Sir Richard Branson summoned Berber to his private island in the Caribbean to seek his advice (along with other global political leaders and business chiefs) on addressing social and environmental issues around the world.

"We wanted to have him there to tap into his unique experience in using business principles to approach social issues in order to drive sustainable results," said a Branson spokeswoman.

Berber has also made Ethiopia something of a family crusade. Every summer, instead of heading to the beach, he packs up his wife and three kids and flies to the Ethiopian outback for several weeks to learn more about the lives and needs of the locals. During a trip in the summer of 2006, the Berbers were greeted like kings in the Ethiopian villages, with thousands of locals surrounding their jeep and holding up signs that read "Thank You Berber!"

Yet while Berber may be getting accolades from Ethiopians and fellow philanthropists, he's proving less popular with the big nonprofits. In fact, he's become their worst nightmare. Through Glimmer, Berber is showing that the wealthy don't need to give money to the United Way, Red Cross, CARE and the rest of the charity establishment. Just as CyBerCorp bypassed the big brokers, Glimmer is proving that today's Richistanis don't need big nonprofits to carry out their good works. The big NGOs, Berber says, are headed toward extinction unless they change their wasteful ways.

"Most NGOs, if they were private companies, would be in bankruptcy," Berber says. "In our lifetime, we're going to see the winds of change and we're going to see donors become more educated about directing their dollars. If anyone knew that some of these charities only spend 19 cents of every dollar on the people they claim to be helping, they would be shocked."

For their part, the charities say Berber is a misguided neophyte who should just stick to software.

"I have no idea how he could arrive at the conclusion that he would better understand the problems of Ethiopia than our organization," says Adam Hicks, a spokesman for CARE. "You have to understand the world context in which Ethiopia exists, to understand deeply the food issues and exporting world. We have people who make it their life study to understand these issues. You can't just go into Ethiopia and say, 'I know everything there is to know about Ethiopia.'" He adds, "CARE staffers are highly trained in what they do. They are agronomists and doctors and engineers. They are more than well-intentioned do-gooders."

Charities like CARE, however, had better get used to people like Phil Berber.

Competitive Altruism

Philip Berber is part of a new generation of philanthropists. Along with giving away record amounts of cash, today's Richistanis are radically changing the way the rich give back to society.

Total charitable giving in the United States has jumped to more than $260 billion—double the level of 1995. Americans with incomes of more than $1 million donated more than $30 billion to charities in 2003, up from $9 billion in 1995, in keeping with their population growth.

Philanthropy has never been more fashionable, with daily announcements about this or that software magnate giving $100 million to his alma mater, or another buyout king giving $20 million for a new museum wing. Honorary plaques now cover countless schools, museums, concert halls and even park benches.

The business press, once leery of rich people bearing gifts, now covers philanthropy like a competitive industry. *BusinessWeek* publishes an annual ranking of the 50 top givers—a kind of Forbes 400 for competitive altruists. *The Wall Street Journal* runs a "Gift of the Week" column, detailing the donations of newly rich hedge funders, deal makers, tech founders and corporate chiefs.

The number of grant-making foundations in the United States has more than doubled since 1990, to more than 67,000. These foundations—used mainly by the wealthy to more personally direct their charitable giving—have assets of more than $500 billion.

Granted, many Richistanis view charity as a cheap way to burnish their image. Others simply want to buy their way into society, and some give because they're discovering that they can't possibly spend their fortunes in their lifetime and don't want to leave a legacy of spoiled children.

Whatever their motives, Richistanis are pouring huge

amounts into philanthropy. Bill Gates's $31 billion foundation is the largest in history—more than five times larger (in 2005 dollars) than the amount given away by the country's previous philanthropic giant, John D. Rockefeller. The Gates Foundation recently got even bigger with Warren Buffet's $31 billion gift in 2006.

Eli Broad, the SunAmerica founder, has given away more than $1.4 billion for public education, arts and science. Michael Dell has pledged more than $1 billion for children's health care, and banker Herbert M. Sandler and his wife, Marion, announced plans to give away almost all of the $2 billion they received from the sale of their California savings and loan in 2006.

Beyond the size of their giving, Richistanis are also changing the way they give. They're no longer content just to hand a check to charity and assume it will be spent wisely. Like Berber they want a say in where their money goes, and they want results. Soup lines and handouts are passé. The new buzzwords are "social profits" and "high-engagement giving."

The shift is due partly to the ineffectiveness of big charities. In 2003, former senator Bill Bradley and consulting firm McKinsey & Co. released a study showing that U.S. charities waste more than $100 billion on fundraising costs and administrative expenses. Other recent studies have found that big foundations have become autocratic, isolated and more focused on self-preservation and fancy offices than on solving global problems.

"There's a greater realization of the inefficiencies of the old organizations," says Ron Perelman, the billionaire financier. "We now have the ability to measure their efficiency and effectiveness and decide where to give."

As a result, Richistanis don't want to create big foundations that last forever. They want to give their money away now, while they can enjoy the praise and control the process. In a 2005 survey of people worth more than $30 million, by Boston College's Center on Wealth and Philanthropy, 65 percent said they planned to donate more of their wealth during their lifetimes than in their estates.

"People realize you can't take it with you," says Sandy Weill, former Citigroup Inc. chief executive and chairman, who has given away $600 million in the past 10 to 15 years. "It's a lot better to do a lot of this philanthropy while you're still alive and you have the energy. We can use our brainpower to make the world a better place now—not to leave a bunch of money that will be around in 100 years. Being the biggest foundation doesn't interest us at all."

The changes are also being driven by the way in which most Richistanis made their fortunes. As we saw in the Third Wave chapter, many of today's biggest fortunes come from the booming financial and technology markets. Richistanis are entrepreneurs, distrustful of institutions and confident of their own abilities to remake markets. They figure that they should be able to give away their money the same way they made it.

Bill Drayton, the management consultant and policy expert who coined the term "social entrepreneur," says that social entrepreneurs play by a different set of rules than the rest of the charity world. They are more like economic revolutionaries than genteel benefactors.

"The job of a social entrepreneur is to recognize when a part of society is stuck and to provide new ways to get it unstuck. He or she finds what is not working and solves the problem by changing the system, spreading the solution and persuading entire societies to take new leaps. Social entrepreneurs are not content just to give a fish or teach how to fish. They will not rest until they have revolutionized the fishing industry."

The top social entrepreneurs include people like Gordon Moore, the Intel cofounder who has pledged more than $7 billion to search for pioneering nature conservation and education projects around the world. Jeff Skoll, a former eBay exec, seeks out entrepreneurial nonprofit leaders and gives them added funding.

Ron Perelman decided to donate millions to an ambitious cancer doctor in California rather than giving to the American Cancer Society or other big foundation. With help from Perelman, the doctor, Dennis Slaman, helped develop Herceptin, which is now widely used in the treatment of breast cancer.

"Sure, there was a risk it wouldn't work out," Perelman said. "But it's like any business or transaction. If the guy has a history of performance and you have confidence in him, you fund it."

The New York–based Robin Hood Foundation, made up mostly of hedge funders, raised $48 million at its annual dinner in 2006 to fight poverty in New York City and holds regular "investor updates" for its givers. It also creates a "portfolio" of groups and causes to fund, based on their risk and missions. Its board of directors funds all the administrative costs, so they can promise that 100 percent of donations go to the people who need it.

Of course, the rise in so-called self-directed giving has also produced its share of follies. Drug-company heiress

Ruth Lilly, for instance, donated $100 million in stock to the Chicago-based Poetry Foundation in 2003. The gift left a small group of reclusive poets to fight over the millions and struggle with new phrases like "portfolio diversification" and "prudent man" theory.

And some venture philanthropists have taken "social profits" to an extreme. Pierre Omidyar, founder of eBay, has folded his charitable Omidyar Foundation into the Omidyar Network, which makes for-profit investments. Omidyar in 2006 gave $100 million in eBay stock to Tufts University for a microfinance program that will lend money to banks, institutional equity funds and other institutions to lend to the poor in developing countries. Tufts is seeking a return on its program of 9 percent or better. The $1 billion foundation set up by Google founders Sergey Brin and Larry Page promises to fight poverty, disease and global warming, while also making profits by funding start-up companies and forming partnerships with venture capitalists.

"After a few years trying to be a traditional philanthropist, I asked myself, if you are doing good, trying to make the world a better place, why limit yourself to non-profit?" Omidyar told *The Economist*.

Charity is also becoming increasingly competitive. Today's rich don't just want to do well by doing good: They want to be the *best* at doing good. Oracle's Larry Ellison, who's pledged to give away more than $600 million, ranks his fellow philanthropists not by how much they've given, but what kind of results that can show.

"Until you start solving problems, until you start curing diseases, until you start delivering results, what difference does it make how much you give?" Ellison said.

Mario Marino, a former software magnate who's become one of the leaders of the venture philanthropy movement, says he's worried that some of today's venture philanthropists may have gone too far. Rich donors, for instance, are increasingly showing up at inner-city community centers and trying to run them like their companies—ignoring the sensitivities and expertise of the staff.

"The typical person from business comes in and thinks he's smarter than these people and thinks he's the savior," Marino says. "And the nonprofit people just think the guy's a greedy, adversarial SOB who would take blood from a turnip. There's still a big gap between the donors and the nonprofits."

Marino says Richistanis, especially those who made their money overnight, tend to overestimate their ability to fix increasingly complex social problems.

"What happens when money comes quickly is that people don't realize that they're not as bright as their money suggests. Too many times people come in with huge egos and try to change the world. I made the mistake myself the first few years, and now I've learned that arrogance is a curse in this field."

Still, control-freak philanthropy is here to stay. And many of its most avid proponents, like Philip Berber, are already using it to address some of society's biggest problems.

Rebel with a Cause

On a Thursday afternoon, Berber is sitting at his conference table swigging a Starbucks. He's annoyed. Even when he's happy, Berber's right eyebrow arches up slightly higher than his left, giving him a look of perpetual surprise. When he gets emotional, the brow arches even higher, becoming a kind of outrage meter. At the moment, he's outraged at the way most of the New Rich go about their philanthropy. And the brow is at full staff.

"When people come into wealth, they're being tested," he says. "Part of having wealth is to be a custodian and guardian for the well-being of our families and those that are our brothers and sisters outside of our countries."

The American rich, he says, have traditionally failed the test. When they give to charity, they're usually doing it to climb the social ladder, win friends, or advance their business interests. Black-tie balls are pure display, he says, and have nothing to do with solving the world's problems.

"I call it dancing for the dollar or feel-good philanthropy. Someone writes a check for their alma mater, after they've been courted and stroked, and they feel good afterward. It's social-ego philanthropy, where you get local praise. You want to be seen donating. There's nothing humble about it; they want to be visible and they want their name on everything. Social-ego philanthropy and feel-good philanthropy are all about responding to requests. That's not what I'm about."

Berber's philanthropic journey began long before he was rich. Born in Dublin to a Jewish clothing maker, Berber grew up with a strong sense of being the outsider and cultural minority. He played on a Jewish soccer team, which would get frequent ribbing from the Catholic opponents.

"It was amusing really," Berber laughs. "Here were

these 11 circumcised Jews playing football against all the Catholics, so you'd get the occasional comment."

When he was a teenager, Berber started realizing that he was different in other ways. Aside from being a math whiz, engineering genius and abstract thinker, he noticed that he processed information much more quickly than his friends. He could look at a printed page and absorb the important facts within seconds. Berber wasn't just a speed-reader; he was a human laser scanner.

"I don't think I've ever finished a book," he says. "I wouldn't need to. I can pick up the important facts just by looking at a page." Berber also rarely watches a movie straight through, since he loses patience.

After college, he worked for a defense contractor (hence, the rocket science), then held a string of corporate jobs in London with Ford, Avon and Bausch & Lomb. Eventually, he struck out on his own and launched companies built on artificial intelligence and financial models. Most of them flopped. Yet one company took off and merged with a Texas company. In 1990, Berber and his wife, who's British, moved to Houston.

"It's safe to say I was the only Irish Jew in Houston," he says.

After a few years, Berber got tired of all the corporate politics and quit. He moved his family to Austin because "at least it was green."

In 1995, he visited one of the first day-trading offices in Houston and realized the business had huge potential. The Internet was just coming of age, and he realized that stock traders could use the Web to trade stocks on their own and break free from the pricey Wall Street brokers.

He stayed up for 24 hours writing a business plan. Within a few months, he launched CyBerCorp.

As day trading exploded, so did CyBerCorp. Berber worked 16-hour days writing trading models and growing the company. From his cramped office in suburban Austin, Berber was mounting a stealthy attack on Merrill Lynch, Smith Barney and the big New York stock exchanges.

"We were taking on Wall Street, we were taking on Nasdaq and shaking the establishment," Berber says. "There was a real rebel spirit in what we were doing. We were getting rid of the expensive, entrenched middlemen and leveling the playing field."

At its peak in 1999 the company had more than $20 million in revenues and more than 150 employees. Berber was involved in almost every aspect of the business, from hiring and marketing to software and lawsuits. "It was all-consuming," he said. "Even when I was home, my wife said I wasn't really home."

In February of 2000, Charles Schwab Corp. offered to buy CyBerCorp for about $450 million in stock. Berber felt the company was worth "maybe half that," so he jumped at the offer. He netted more than $220 million. His timing was perfect: The Internet crashed weeks later, and electronic-trading stocks plummeted. Even though he was paid in Schwab stock, Berber sold the bulk of his holdings before it hit bottom.

"After 20 years, I became an overnight success," he says.

Berber promised to stay at the company at least a year to help with the transition. The same night he sold CyBer-Corp, however, his new career as a venture philanthropist was already unfolding.

Just before midnight on February 1, 2000, Berber was sitting in his hotel room in New York, putting the final touches on the deal, when his wife, Donna, burst in the room. She had just spent the day at the Ethiopian embassy in Washington, D.C., meeting with the country's charity liaison. The Berbers had been fascinated by Ethiopia ever since 1985, when they attended the Band-Aid rock concert at Wembley Stadium to benefit Ethiopian famine victims. The images of emaciated children, and the role that organizer Bob Geldof played in raising awareness for the cause, inspired the Berbers. They promised themselves that if they ever came into money, Ethiopia would be their number one cause.

In 1999, after selling some shares of private stock in the company, the Berbers set aside $200,000 to fund an orphanage in Ethiopia. When Donna visited the embassy to work out the details, she met a man named Tameru Abasaba—a learned aid expert who came from one of the poorest regions of Ethiopia. Tameru's job at the embassy was to coordinate aid by Americans to Ethiopia.

During the meeting, both Tameru and Donna cried as they talked about the 1980s famine. Tameru told her that creating an orphanage was a nice idea, but that the Ethiopians really needed clean water and health care.

Tameru recalls: "I said to Donna 'Just go there and see for yourself. Ask the Ethiopians what they need. Then decide.' "

Donna flew to Addis Ababa and spent several days handing out bread and clothes to crowds of sick children huddled on the streets of the city.

"My whole world opened up," Donna recalls. "I had no frame of reference in my own mind, so to show up and to see that kind of suffering and despair and problems that were so vast in nature, it changed my perspective. At the same time that these people were suffering, they were also so dignified and proud."

Philip made his own trip to Ethiopia a few months later and was equally transformed.

"When I came back from Ethiopia, I knew that my days of working for a living, of being a corporate entrepreneur were numbered," he says. "It totally changed my thinking."

Berber resigned in late 2000, and he and Donna decided to commit $100 million in Schwab stock to Glimmer. While the Berbers still live very comfortably—they charter planes, have a big house and drive a silver Ferrari—they plan to give even more of their fortune away as time goes on.

"For Donna and me, we didn't come from this American materialistic thing. For me this work seemed much more fulfilling than hoarding dollars the rest of our lives."

Still, Berber wasn't ready to abandon his tech-start-up business impulses. His whole life had been built around financial-trading models, Internet software, scalability and return on assets. He was a dyed-in-the-wool entrepreneur, always looking for cheaper, faster ways of delivering products or services. For Berber, efficiency was king. And he wasn't about to give it up for some touchy-feely notion of philanthropy.

"There was nothing philanthropic about dot-coms and day trading," he says. "Donna started this journey from the heart. For me it was still about my head."

So Berber decided to give away his fortune the same way he made it—by following his business instincts. He created a business plan, wrote a mission statement and set "profit targets" and goals. At first, the Ethiopians didn't know what to make of Berber's corporate zeal. Some local NGOs that he tried working with refused, saying they couldn't follow all the strict rules. Others didn't believe Berber would make good on his promises.

"They said I was way too young to have so much money to give away," Berber said. "They didn't think I really had it."

In launching Glimmer, Berber came up with his own set of rules. They are, he says, basic principles of business that any philanthropist can apply to charitable giving. Here are the top five Berber's Rules:

1. **Know Your Customer.** Berber began Glimmer like all his other businesses, with intensive research. He pored over dozens of tomes on agriculture, disease and Ethiopian culture. He scanned studies on education, the history of poverty, African politics and global weather patterns. He talked to other aid groups to find out what they were doing and what causes were being overlooked.

His best research, however, came from the Ethiopians themselves.

"We went to the poorest villages and asked the people what they most wanted," Berber says. "Ethiopians may be poor, but they're not stupid. I'm sorry to say that the bulk of international aid starts in an ivory tower somewhere in Washington or wherever and then the ex-pats tell the Africans what it is they need and want."

Berber discovered that what the Ethiopians wanted most was clean water. So he built wells. After that, they wanted schools, so he built schools. After that, they wanted jobs, so he launched an innovative program for farmers that would increase their incomes and demand for labor.

Berber acknowledges he can't know everything about Ethiopia's problems. That's why he hired Tameru—the Ethiopian NGO expert—to run Glimmer of Hope's office in Addis Ababa.

"You hire the best domain expertise, just like in business," he says.

2. **Cut Costs, Remove the Middleman.** Berber is obsessive about costs. His first act as a philanthropist was to read Graham Hancock's book *The Lords of Poverty,* an exposé on the corruption, exploitation and inefficiency of nongovernmental organizations (NGOs). The book convinced him that if he wanted to help Ethiopians, he had to do it himself.

At some charities, less than 50 cents of every dollar donated went to the poor, he learned. The rest of the money went to bureaucracies and bloated overhead. When he went to Africa, he often saw highly paid Western aid workers driving around in shiny Range Rovers and sending their kids to top private schools—all paid for by donors who thought they were giving to the poor. On a flight to Ethiopia once, Berber sat next to a World Bank worker who was flying first class. Berber asked the man what he was doing in Ethiopia.

"He said he was traveling there to write a report. Why was this guy flying first class to produce some 300-page report?"

Berber calls Glimmer a "secure pipeline" or "direct aid," like Dell's "direct-sales" model for personal computers.

He employs only about a dozen people in cramped offices in Austin, London and Addis Ababa (his charity also funds projects in the United Kingdom and Texas). He doesn't have any sales, marketing or fund-raising costs, since he funds Glimmer himself.

Once the money gets to Africa, Berber has a streamlined bidding process that further reduces costs and limits corruption. Like a money manager, Glimmer "allocates" a certain amount to each of the country's regions. Glimmer's regional partners—small, local NGOs—then ask Ethiopians in all the villages about their most pressing needs. Next, the NGOs send a proposal to Glimmer along with a simple spreadsheet, which Berber can compare with other NGOs. Glimmer personnel also make frequent site visits to check the work.

"If an NGO in one region says it will cost $162 per head to build a school, and we're building one nearby for $63, we won't fund it," Berber says. "If someone's way out of line on costs, that's a sign of corruption."

3. **Hold Them Accountable.** Berber has performance targets built into every grant he makes. When he funds a small NGO in Ethiopia, he pays it only for the first quarter. If it achieves its goals—digging a certain number of wells, or starting a school—he funds the NGO a second quarter. If it doesn't, it loses the funding.

At first, the Ethiopian NGOs resented the process. They saw it as overly demanding and punitive. Berber says almost half the groups Glimmer funds don't make it past the first or second quarters. Now, he says, most of the groups are used to it.

"These developing nations have become dependent on

handouts," he says. "Grants became an entitlement. There is no trust, either of the donors or of the recipients. We're trying to change that."

At the same time, Berber has cut down on paperwork. Big charities thrive on reports. Berber hates them. Rather than asking the NGOs he funds to send lengthy details on their work, Berber demands concise, two-page summaries and one-page spreadsheets.

"People would give us these thick reports and we'd push them back," Berber says. "If we had enough people to read the reports, we wouldn't have money to go to the people."

The reports are filed quarterly, so Berber can spot problems quickly. He also holds weekly teleconferences with the entire staff. "If the wheels are coming off a project, I want to know about it as soon as possible."

It's taken years for Ethiopians to get used to Berber's reporting process. But now he works with 10 or 12 small NGOs who have adopted his system.

4. **Involve Your Customers.** Too many charity projects in Africa end up dying from neglect. The donors lose interest and the recipients lose initiative. Berber says the secret to long-term success—known as "sustainability" in charity speak—is to involve the local Ethiopians from the very beginning.

"We buy the bricks, they build a wall. We buy the pipe, they dig the trench."

For water wells, for instance, Berber helped set up local water committees that can manage the wells and fix them when they break. Wells built by international

NGOs, by contrast, are often left in disrepair because the locals don't have the parts for repairs.

5. **Leverage Your Dollars.** In business, Berber learned the power of leverage—piggybacking on other people's money to increase your own returns. Glimmer uses leverage by funding the local NGOs in Ethiopia, who already get some funding from the Ethiopian government. The groups get Glimmer's money, and Glimmer gets the NGOs' local expertise.

It's also starting to work with international aid. Last year, Berber started thinking about how to create economic development and higher wages in Ethiopia. He started researching the country's largest market—millions of farmers who live on a dollar a day or less. He came up with the idea of buying an irrigation pump and allowing farmers to buy it with a seven-year, no-interest loan. He found a test group of farmers in the remote town of Adina Fas, in the province of Tigray. At first, the Ethiopians were reluctant to pay for something that would benefit them years later. But Berber prevailed. Farmers who once got one crop a year now get two. Their average income, which was once $110 a year, has soared to $1,200.

The European Union was so impressed with the results that it gave a grant to the province of Tigray to fund 200 more of Berber's irrigation systems.

"We're sowing the seeds of social capital," he says. "I can't solve Africa's problems. But maybe I can deal with one little patch of the quilt, and if we get that right, other people will replicate it."

Berber admits there are times when his rigorous business model breaks down for charities. The morning after the Asian tsunami in 2004, he and his family sat around the breakfast table and decided to donate $1 million to the cause. The trouble was, Philip couldn't find a charity that met his tests for efficiency and business focus. It took him three weeks, and hours and hours of research to find a few relief groups that he was comfortable funding.

"The impulse to give was open-hearted but then the head kicked in," he says. "If I just wanted to give away the money to feel good, I could have given to the Red Cross. But the social investor in me had to do my homework."

Berber recognizes that he's invented a career that has never really existed. He's not a member of the "idle rich," or a traditional philanthropist. And he's not really an entrepreneur, since he gives away money. His business card simply reads "Philip Berber—Glimmer of Hope." When people ask him what he does for a living, he usually fudges the answer.

"I really struggle with that," he says. "I wish I had a quick word people understood. Philanthropist? I can hardly spell the word. Humanitarian? That's too high-falutin'. If I say charity work, that's wrong, too. If I say social entrepreneur or social investor, people say, 'Oh, you're a banker?' So I'm kind of at a loss on that one."

In the end, Berber just hopes he can make a difference in a part of the world that needs it most. And, perhaps in the process, he hopes to lead the way to a new brand of philanthropy.

"What's my legacy?" he says. "I don't know. I guess I don't ask to be remembered for anything. My needs are more simple than that. We do what we can during this lifetime for the well-being of those who are less fortunate. When I'm six feet under and lying in a box . . . legacy, shmegacy, it doesn't matter. I'm enjoying what I'm doing in this lifetime, and if I helped a few people and set a good example for my children, that would be great."

MOVE OVER, CHRISTIAN COALITION

The New Political Kingmakers

For more than 40 years, the Colorado legislature was dominated by Republicans.

The GOP, rooted in the state's Wild West libertarianism and backed by local oil magnates, ranchers and corporate chiefs, was synonymous with the Colorado Establishment. The party controlled the state House and Senate since the 1960s, with only brief victories by the Democrats. By 2004, with George W. Bush on his way to carrying the state a second time, the Colorado Republicans seemed invincible. (The Democratic sweep of Congress in 2006 was still years away.)

"There was a mind-set that we couldn't lose," says Alan Philp, a Republican strategist in Colorado. "There was a sense that the Democrats didn't have the resources or potential to take the legislature."

Then, along came the Gang of Four.

In the early fall of 2004, the state was suddenly flooded with mailings, TV ads and radio spots attacking Republican candidates. Ray Martinez, a popular Republican candidate for the state Senate in Fort Collins, came home one day to find a mailer that showed him peeping into a woman's bedroom. "Ray Martinez wants to control what goes on in your bedroom," the pamphlet said, criticizing his staunch pro-life stance. Another mailing portrayed him lounging on the beach in Florida and said he was taking vacations on the taxpayer dime. (As the Fort Collins mayor, he had gone to Florida for a mayors' conference.)

Other Republican candidates faced similar broadsides. A TV commercial targeting Republican U.S. Representative Marilyn Musgrave showed an overweight blonde in a pink suit stealing a watch from a corpse, picking the pockets of U.S. soldiers in Iraq and dunking a family in toxic waste—highlighting Musgrave's positions on soldier pay and environmental issues. Other TV and radio ads accused local Republicans of bowing to extremist ideologues who cared more about pushing a Christian agenda than fixing the state's more pressing problems like education, health care and jobs.

The messages struck a chord with voters. On November 3, Coloradans handed the GOP a stunning defeat. Martinez and others, who had strong leads before the advertising blitz, were handily defeated. In the Senate, the GOP's one-vote majority swung to a one-vote Democratic advantage. More surprisingly, the Democrats picked up seven seats in the House, giving them control. It was the first time the Democrats ruled both houses since 1961.

The Republicans had been outspent by three to one in many races. In the Martinez race alone, the opponents spent a record $1 million or more to Martinez's $350,000. In a state where the GOP had always been the party of the rich and powerful, party leaders scrambled to figure out where all this new, Democratic money was coming from. Campaign filings showed the funds came from four organizations—the Coalition for a Better Colorado, Forward Colorado, Alliance for a Better Colorado and Alliance for Colorado Families. No one had ever heard of the groups, which were all 527s—the lightly regulated advocacy groups that can pour unlimited amounts of money into elections.

Even more surprising was the fact that the vast majority of the funding for the groups came from just four individuals. They were all Coloradans and they were all very rich. Three of them were self-made tech entrepreneurs, and one was the billionaire heiress of a medical-device fortune. While they had all been active in state politics over the years, they had never teamed up to transform an important election. The Republicans branded them "the Gang of Four," and accused them of forming a cabal so rich and powerful that they could buy elections.

"These four individuals had a huge impact," Philp told me. "They were very focused, they had a goal and they executed it. There is little doubt that legislators and candidates in the state of Colorado are wary of getting on the wrong side of these folks."

The Gang included Jared Polis, a 32-year-old dot-com

whiz who's already created and sold several tech companies and has a net worth estimated at more than $200 mil-
lion. It included Tim Gill, a former software magnate
who's worth more than $400 million and who's become
the nation's top funder of gay-rights causes. Rounding out
the group was Pat Stryker, the billionaire heiress to the
Stryker medical-device fortune, and Rutt Bridges, a geo-
physicist who made his money creating software for oil
exploration and had a fortune worth tens of millions.

They came from vastly different backgrounds and
ideologies. Yet they united around one big idea—to create
greater opportunities for all Coloradans. They wanted
more money spent on education, health care and job creation. In contrast to wealthy Republicans, who often ad-
vocated less government and lower taxes (especially for
the rich), the Gang of Four wanted more public support
for the less fortunate. As Bridges told a local newspaper,
"There are reasons as a society we support public func-
tions. We seem to be losing that. There's this attitude we
have to lower taxes and have less government."

Of course, the members of the Gang of Four were acting
partly out of self-interest. Bridges and Polis were both considering a run for higher political office, while Gill, who's
openly gay, had a personal stake in leading the crusade
for gay rights. Yet through their 2004 campaign and their
continued efforts, the Gang of Four is trying to create a
new kind of rich-man's politics. Rather than trying to use
government to make themselves richer—through lower
taxes or special handouts for their businesses—they see
government as a tool for more progressive agendas. While
their campaign has gone largely unnoticed beyond Colorado,

the Gang of Four may signal a broader, national shift in the politics of the wealthy.

Learjet Liberals

The American wealth boom has created a new generation of rich activists. Whether they're funding campaigns or running for office, Richistanis are emerging as a major force in American politics. They've conquered the business world, and now they want power.

They come from all points along the political spectrum. For every left-leaning George Soros there's a right-leaning T. Boone Pickens. Yet it's the rich Democrats who are having the greatest impact—and not just because of the recent GOP crisis in Washington. The enormous wealth created in the nation's liberal knowledge capitals—New York, California, Seattle, Austin, Denver, Boston and Washington—has spawned a new generation of left-leaning millionaires and billionaires. Many also grew up during the 1960s, during a time of increased sensitivity to minorities and the underclass. These "Learjet liberals," to use author Jonathan Rauch's term, are challenging the stereotype of rich politicos who see government as a tool to advance their wealth. Instead, they're using their wealth as a tool to advance government.

Some are running for office. The number of candidates spending more than $1 million of their own money on their campaigns has soared from an average of three a year in the 1980s and 1990s to 24 in the 2004 election. Jon Corzine, a former Goldman Sachs exec, spent $61 million of his own money to win a U.S. Senate seat and several million dollars to become New Jersey's governor. Michael Bloomberg, the financial-information magnate whose positions on social issues are more Democratic than Republican, spent $74 million to become New York City's mayor, and another $77 million to get reelected (that works out to be about $100 per vote). Democrat Maria Cantwell spent nearly $10 million of her own fortune to win a Senate seat in the state of Washington, and Wisconsin Democrat Herb Kohl spent nearly $5 million of his own to retain his Senate seat.

Jennifer Steen, a political science professor at Boston College and the author of *Self-Financed Candidates in Congressional Elections*, says that loans and contributions from candidates increased from $36.6 million in 1990 to $124.7 million in 2004. With campaigns becoming so expensive, and fund-raising becoming more restricted because of campaign-finance laws, politics has increasingly become a battle of millionaire versus millionaire.

The richest of the New Rich candidates tend to be Democrats. A study by Steen showed that among candidates who spent more than $4 million on their campaigns—what Steen calls "super extreme self-financers"—Democrats outnumber Republicans by three to one. Among "kind-of-extreme self-financiers," or those who spend $1 million to $4 million, Republicans outnumber Democrats by almost two to one. In other words, the Republicans may rule Lower Richistan, but the Dems rule the top.

The trend also holds true for voters. A survey done by wealth researcher Russ Alan Prince during the 2004 elections showed that most single-digit millionaires backed President Bush in the 2004 election, citing his tax cuts and other "pocketbook" issues. The majority of superrich voters, or those worth $10 million or more, supported John Kerry, saying they cared more about the environment, budget deficits, health care and education, which were seen as Kerry issues.

Prince says the study shows that the superrich are more accustomed to thinking long term, over several generations. Just as they plan their estates and investments to last 100 years (because they can), they also view politics as a longer-term proposition. They don't have to vote from their pocketbooks, since their pocketbooks are already fat enough. They're more concerned with global warming, the failing U.S. education system and ailing health-care system—issues that will more likely affect their grandchildren.

"At a certain level of wealth, you care more about things like the environment and what's going to happen to later generations than preserving your own money," Prince says.

These aren't the guilt-ridden "limousine liberals" of old, who arrived at their political views largely out of embarrassment over their unearned riches. Richistanis made their money themselves and they want to preserve the system of fairness and opportunities they had growing up. They see government more like an extension of their philanthropy—a way to leverage their charitable dollars to bring about greater social change. They have spent millions to fight poverty, improve the environment, fix inner cities and cure disease. And they're now realizing that all their philanthropic donations are a drop in the bucket compared with government spending in the same areas.

As one education philanthropist told me, "When you look at what I spend compared to what government spends on schools, it's like pissing in the wind." So to have impact, today's philanthropists also want a say in directing government funds.

Bill Gates, for instance, has donated more than $100 million to help improve New York City schools. Yet Michael Bloomberg, who spent even more to get elected as New York mayor, has exerted greater influence by helping to direct the city's $12 billion school budget.

"To the mayor, politics is seen as a highly effective form of philanthropy," says one aide (though some opponents and teachers' unions, of course, might disagree).

There are still plenty of Richistanis who want to use government to get richer. More than a dozen wealthy families—including the Gallos of wine-making fame, and the Mars candy clan—have lobbied successfully for a reduction in the estate tax. In his book *Wealth and Democracy*, Kevin Phillips argues that the American rich have consistently corrupted politicians and manipulated government to reap larger fortunes, especially during wealth booms.

"The essence of plutocracy, fulfilled in 2000," Phillips writes, "has been the determination and ability of wealth to reach beyond its own realm of money and control politics and government as well. In America, explains political scientist Samuel Huntington, 'money becomes evil not when it is used to buy goods but when it is used to buy power . . . economic inequalities become evil when they are translated into political inequalities.'"

Yet the stories of Jared Polis and Tim Gill offer another, more hopeful sign for the effect of wealth on politics.

Nuking the GOP

Jared Polis is late for lunch. Snatching his Dell laptop from his desk, the bespectacled millionaire races out the door of his third-floor office in downtown Boulder. It's a sunny September day, with the jagged Rockies soaring to a crystal-blue sky. Polis doesn't notice the weather. Dressed in a golf shirt, Dockers and hiking boots, he's glued to his cell phone as he speed-walks to his apartment a few blocks away.

He arrives to a crowd of about a dozen people waiting in his living room. Polis's home is more Tribeca than Boulder, filled with brushed steel, tubular lamps and ankle-high sofas. A huge fish tank filled with coral and angelfish glows in the entryway, and the living room is dominated by a giant flat-screen TV and four leather lounge chairs. Dozens of shiny copper pots hang from the ceiling kitchen, though Polis later acknowledges, "They're mainly for show. I don't really have time to cook."

The people gathered are all friends and family of Jared's. Most are rich Democrats. They include David Friedman, a prominent fund-raiser and owner of a chain of extended-care homes in New England. One of the founders of PayPal is there, along with two other tech mavens, a finance entrepreneur and Brad Feld, a top venture capitalist, wearing jeans and a T-shirt.

Jared's parents, Susan and Stephen Schutz, whom Jared describes as "classic hippies," also stop by. (Jared uses his mother's maiden name "Polis," because he says he "liked the sound of it better.") This afternoon, Susan, who has purple-streaked hair, is wearing a tangerine-colored scarf and dark sunglasses.

The lunch, like most Polis events, has a political purpose—to raise money for Colorado's Democratic candidate for governor, Bill Ritter. Ritter, a square-jawed, highly polished former district attorney, is critical to the Democrats' hopes in Colorado. If he wins, the Democrats will control all three branches of state government for the first time since 1961. Jared has hosted or cohosted fund-raisers that have raised more than $300,000 for Ritter. And he's donated thousands of dollars to various Democratic legislators. Today's lunch raises about $10,000.

The group talks about the environment, technology, tourism and business and gently prods the governor to stay clear of religious issues while in government. At the end of the lunch, Polis makes a request for the group to donate more time and money to the Democrats. "They need our help," he says. "If you haven't given the maximum allowable, please do. And you can still give up to $2,500 to the party, which can also help Ritter. So I would urge you to take a look at how much you've given and see if you could do more."

Polis looks at the clock, realizes he's late for his next meeting and dashes out the door.

"I don't know where he gets all his energy," says his mother. "It sure didn't come from us."

Polis does credit his parents for his entrepreneurial zeal, which has made him one of the youngest tech tycoons in America. His mom and dad are self-described "flower children" who protested Vietnam and traveled the country in the late 1960s selling homemade posters from the back of a pickup truck. They formed a company called

Blue Mountain Arts and started publishing poetry books. She wrote the poems; her husband did the artwork. When a few of the books became bestsellers, they moved to an up-scale neighborhood near San Diego, where Jared grew up.

Even at a young age, Polis had a knack for making money. In high school, he started a scrap-metal trading firm that bought old jeeps and shell casings from the Department of Defense and sold them to steel mills. He also sold tomatoes from a roadside stand, helped his parents as a salesman for Blue Mountain and spent a summer in Russia trading privatization vouchers on the Russian Commodities Exchange.

He also loved politics. When he was 11, a local developer announced plans to build homes around a canyon that Jared and his brother used as their daily playground. Jared overheard his parents talking about the plans and asked to go to a city council meeting to oppose the plans. He stood up and gave a rousing speech opposing the project, and convinced the town council to scale back the development.

"That was when he realized he could have an impact on public policy," says his younger brother, Jorian.

Polis founded a Young Democrats Club in high school and at 13 volunteered on Senator Alan Cranston's reelection campaign. He always had a soft spot for kids; one day in high school he brought home a dozen Mexican orphans whom he'd agreed to house for a night as part of his work with the Spanish Language Club.

"Mom was pretty surprised when I showed up with these orphans," he recalls. "But she let them stay."

Polis finished high school early and went to Princeton at age 16. Even with a double course load, he found time to team up with two friends to start American Information

Systems (AIS), an Internet service provider in Chicago. He spent most of his senior year flying to Chicago, raising financing and running the business. They sold it a few years later for $20 million. In 1996, he and his parents formed an offshoot of Blue Mountain called BlueMountain.com, which made digital greeting cards. At the height of the dot-com bubble in 1999, Polis and his family sold the business to Excite@Home for more than $700 million, despite the company's lack of profits (it was later resold for less than $40 million). Meantime, Polis launched Provide Commerce, whose ProFlowers service cut the price of sending flowers by allowing customers to purchase directly from growers over the Internet. Polis sold that company in 2005 for more than $450 million.

For all his riches, Polis has a decidedly low-key lifestyle. Aside from his loft, which he calls his "one extravagance," he has small apartments in Denver and Manhattan. He avoids the Aspen scene, rarely travels and says he usually flies commercial. His offices in Boulder and Denver are jammed with staffers who work for his various foundations, start-up companies, personal investment firms and nonprofit groups—all under the unofficial umbrella of Jared Polis Inc. He does most of his work in the passenger seat of his Lexus hybrid SUV, typing away on his laptop and cell phone, while his driver, Mark, speeds him from meeting to meeting.

"I don't know, maybe it's ADD (attention deficit disorder), but I like to be involved in a lot of different things," he says.

He says he rarely stresses out, since "getting stressed is nonproductive and I avoid things that are nonproductive." Even his leisure time is results driven: When he watches movies at home, he taps out e-mails on his laptop. "I figure that I'm only 25 percent productive when I'm watching a movie, but I can still get a lot done." He says he does most of his book reading in the shower.

"I take 30-minute showers, which is pretty long. All the pages get wet, so you can tell which books I've read in my house because they're all puffy from the water."

Polis's central political issue is education. The wealth boom of the last decade, he says, has left out too many Americans and improving the education system is the best way to help level the playing field.

"For me, it's all about opportunity, and how to bring it to all Americans so they can succeed," he says. "To give them a chance to reach their potential."

Polis has launched a chain of charter schools, called the New America Schools, for immigrants who are struggling to learn English and go to school at night after work. He served on the Colorado Board of Education until 2007, funds a teacher award program, publishes an education newsletter and has helped campaign for several bond issues to fund school expansions.

Polis's ultimate goal is to run for political office, probably Congress. To get there, he'll have to overcome his rich-kid, smarter-than-thou image, as well as his occasional discomfort in social situations. During a visit to his charter school one morning, he popped into a class and introduced himself to a startled Mexican teenager.

"Hi, I'm Jared Polis. I started this school," Polis said, holding out his hand for a shake.

"Oh. Okay, cool," the boy said, staring blankly at Polis's hand.

Polis's personal life may also become a barrier to higher

office, especially among conservative Colorado voters. This year, after persistent rumors about his personal life, Polis announced to a Boulder newspaper that he is gay. Polis says, "I've always felt my personal life is personal. I think sexual orientation, like religion or race, has nothing to do with one's values, and to most people it's not important one way or the other."

Polis has also proven that money talks in politics. His career as an elected official began in 2000, when he decided to run for the state's Board of Education. The Board of Ed's at-large seat has always been one of the more mundane elected offices in Colorado—somewhere between county commissioner and state legislator. Races for the seat were low-budget affairs, costing a few thousand dollars. Polis spent more than $1 million on the race. He bought a yellow school bus, loaded it with computers and tech gear and traveled the state to campaign and teach children about technology. He bought ads, put up signs and sent out mailings. He shipped 63 bouquets of flowers to the state's 63 Democratic county chairmen. Polis's opponent, former state senator Ben Alexander, says he spent about $7,000. Yet Polis won by a razor-thin margin of less than 100 votes, out of 1.5 million ballots cast.

"At one point," Alexander said, "when I heard he was willing to spend $1 million, I thought of writing him a letter saying 'Let's split it in half, you give me $500,000 and I promise, I'll drop out.' I never sent it, but I wish I had."

It was just the beginning of the Polis money machine. Over the next few years, Polis gave generously to Democratic causes and candidates. He created $1,000 awards for teachers, contributed to soft-money committees and funded liberal Web sites. It was all a prelude to his greatest contribution—as a founding member of the Gang of Four.

A Band of Brothers

The group began with a lunch. Al Yates, the retired president of Colorado State University and one of the state's most powerful and distinguished African Americans, sat down in the spring of 2003 with his friend Ken Salazar, then the state's attorney general. The two had grown increasingly frustrated with the state's leadership. Colorado's education system was faltering. Its health-care system was a mess. Job growth had slowed following the technology and telecom bust of 2001 and 2002. The Republicans in the legislature and governor's office were spending much of their time waging an ideological crusade against the Left, introducing bills targeting liberal college professors and pushing legislation banning the discussion of homosexuality in the classroom. They also backed a resolution to support a federal constitutional amendment to ban gay marriage.

Salazar and Yates wanted change. They knew they couldn't rely on the existing political establishment, so they decided to try to create a political movement of their own.

They started holding informal meetings with leading Democratic thinkers and businesspeople. The group didn't talk about specific policies, but rallied around broad values associated with "progressive politics"—social justice, fairness and creating greater opportunity for even the poorest Coloradans. Rutt Bridges was one of the first members.

Also onboard was Pat Stryker, a low-profile mom who is worth an estimated $1.4 billion from her stake in her family's medical-supply company, Stryker Corp.

In early 2004, Yates called Tim Gill, a tall, lanky computer geek who made more than $400 million during the tech boom. Gill had devoted millions to antidiscrimination measures for gays and lesbians around the country, so when the Denver legislature started becoming a hotbed of antigay legislation, Gill vowed revenge.

"My philosophy during the 2004 election cycle was 'punish the wicked,'" he says, sitting in his art-deco mansion across from the Denver Country Club. "I wanted to stop all the antigay bills from going through."

Gill wasn't always so hostile to the GOP. Descended from a long line of Colorado Republicans, including Ted Gill, a famous Colorado Republican legislator in the 1950s and 1960s, Gill believes passionately in free markets and fiscal conservatism. He admits to "terrible libertarian tendencies," adding, "I tend to believe you should support people in succeeding but you shouldn't take away their ability to fail. Failure is an integral part of learning to succeed."

Gill's rise to riches also fits the Republican mold. He grew up in an upper-middle-class home outside Denver, with a father who was a successful plastic surgeon and a mom who was a homemaker. A math whiz and computer addict, Gill worked on computers in high school and taught himself programming. Yet as a gay man growing up in Denver in the 1970s, Gill felt like a social outcast. "In gym class, I got picked after the fat kid."

When Gill told his parents he was gay, during his freshman year at University of Colorado–Boulder, his mother was traumatized. "She told me, 'If your father's colleagues ever find out, his career will be at an end,'" Gill recalls. She went to therapy and ended up reading so many self-help books that she got a master's in psychology and started her own practice.

Tim graduated from college and went to work for Hewlett-Packard to work on the earliest personal computers. After growing frustrated with corporate life, he borrowed $2,000 from his parents and launched a publishing-software company in his spare bedroom. The company, called Quark, grew to more than $300 million a year in revenues by the late 1980s.

In 1992, he decided to sell his 50 percent stake in Quark to his business partner and retire.

"I had made myself a lot of promises along the way. First I promised that I would retire when I had $5 million. Then I promised I would retire when I turned 35. I kept breaking my promises. So finally I made a promise to myself that I would retire when I had a half-billion dollars to give away. I felt I couldn't break the promise because I thought I could never get there."

When he decided to sell out, Gill's partner agreed to buy his stake for $300 million, leaving Gill with accumulated wealth of more than $400 million. Since money usually grows with investment returns, he realized he had reached his goal and retired to start a foundation.

In the beginning, Gill steered clear of politics. He was friendly with both Republicans and Democrats, and he focused primarily on gay-rights issues, which at the time were seen as less partisan. "We viewed politics as evil and dirty," he says. In 1992, he spent $30,000 to try to stop an amendment in Colorado that would have prevented cities like Denver from enacting laws to protect the rights of gay citizens. The amendment passed, and Gill decided to re-double his efforts to fund gay-rights bills.

"You want to leave the world a better place and I don't expect the average straight millionaire to say 'I want to make this my issue.' So if it's not my issue, whose is it going to be?"

His goals of funding gay rights and remaining non-partisan became mutually exclusive after the election of George W. Bush in 2000. The Colorado Republicans, like the national GOP, became closely aligned with the Christian Right and family-values groups, who openly opposed homosexuality. Gill was smack in the middle of the Christian movement, since his foundation was based in Colorado Springs—home to Focus on the Family and Ted Haggard, the former head of the National Association of Evangelicals, who railed against gay marriage (Haggard resigned in 2006 after admitting to hiring a male prostitute). Gill realized that being apolitical was no longer a choice.

"I had always given money to both Democrats and Republicans. In the end, this country is 50-50, Democrat and Republican, so you're never going to get your way unless you have bipartisan support. Our idea was, let's find the good Republicans and good Democrats and give them money. But after Bush got into power, the number of Republicans willing to accept money of that kind dried up. There are still good Republicans and we still give money to them. But the social conservatives have such a hammerlock on the Republican Party that the whole strategy of making friends with Republicans would no longer work. My philosophy became, if you can't make friends with people in the Republican Party, then you've got to get rid of the worst ones."

So when Al Yates called in 2003 to ask him to help oust the Republicans, Gill was all ears. Yates and Stryker flew to Gill's house in Aspen for lunch and Gill instantly signed on. A short time later, Yates and Bridges invited Polis to dinner at the Fort Collins Country Club, and Polis became the group's chief strategist.

They made for an unlikely team. Polis, the ambitious, high-profile upstart, was a self-described moderate who wanted to keep friends on both sides of the political aisle. Gill was more personally reserved, but took a no-holds-barred approach to getting rid of the Republicans and promoting gay rights. Bridges, a centrist, was also considering political office and wanted to maintain his Republican relationships. Stryker, a down-to-earth divorced mother of three, was focused on family issues and "social justice." Although she was the group's biggest funder, she was also the most silent, designating Yates as her representative for their meetings.

"Early on, we knew that the only way to create something meaningful was to set aside our special agendas," Yates says. "We didn't talk about specific policies and we avoided the emotional issues."

In the end, the group had one unifying goal: ousting the Republicans.

By election day, they had plowed more than $3 million into the election effort. For state races, the group spent more than $2 million, about twice the amount spent by Republican groups. They also bankrolled ads against Republicans running for national office. Coloradans for Plain Talk, backed by Gill, Polis and Stryker, spent $1 million on the ads targeting Musgrave, who had sponsored federal legislation to amend the Constitution to ban same-sex marriage. At the height of the ad blitz, Musgrave blasted an e-mail to church groups pleading for support against a "radical homosexual agenda."

"Leaders of the homosexual lobby know if they can take me out, no one will stand against them in the future," she wrote in a mass e-mail to conservative Christian groups. Musgrave won, but only by a slim margin.

Republican state senator Jim Dyer—also an enemy of Gill's—was another key target. A TV ad highlighted a real-estate deal in which Dyer bought a home for $10 from an 83-year-old woman with Alzheimer's disease. (Dyer was later forced by a court to pay restitution.) Pam Rhodes, a Republican candidate in nearby Adams County, was leading in polls until a flood of mailings were sent out that described her as a right-wing extremist.

Aside from funding ads, the group recruited Democrats to run for office. Being a Democrat in the Colorado legislature had become a dead-end career path, since their bills were often quashed by the Republicans. The Gang of Four scouted for bright, aspiring Democrats and helped fund their campaigns. They also funded negative ad campaigns against up-and-coming conservatives, to stop them before they became powerful.

"Marilyn Musgrave started on the school board," Gill says. "She would have been so much cheaper to nuke when she was on the school board or even when she was in the legislature. We need to be vigilant and find politicians who are bad and stop them when it's cheap rather than allowing them to get into an expensive position."

Still, Polis and Gill say the money spent by the Gang of Four was only one factor in the elections. The elections,

Polis insists, were mostly a result of voter discontent with the Republicans.

"It was more about what the Republicans *didn't* do," Polis says. "They weren't dealing with any of the problems the state faced, like the huge budget deficit."

Yet pollsters and Republicans say the Gang of Four was largely responsible for the 2004 upset.

"They all came together and they had a profound effect," said Floyd Ciruli, a Denver-based independent pollster. "But for them, the Democrats wouldn't have won." By 2006, the Colorado Republicans had regrouped and formed a Gang of their own. Oil magnate Bruce Benson and beer maker Pete Coors teamed up to fund the Trailhead Group, a 527 that supported local candidates and planned to spend at least $4 million in the elections. Still, the Republicans lag Democrats when it comes to millionaire check writers.

"We have a lot of success in getting people to write checks in the $25,000 to $100,000 range," Philp says. "But when you start talking about seven-figure checks, we don't have that kind of success. There are plenty of Republicans who are New Wealth, but I think the Democrats who are New Wealth seem to have been more politically motivated so far."

Indeed, in the 2006 race, the Colorado Democrats strengthened their majority in the legislature. Ritter won the governor's post. Gill suffered a slight setback when a state domestic-partnership law was voted down, but he was encouraged that 12 of the 13 "antigay" candidates that he opposed in Colorado were defeated.

As for the future, Gill echoes the famous Bush phrase: "I plan to stay the course."

10

WORRIED WEALTH

The Trouble with Money

According to a 2005 study, less than half of today's Richistanis agreed with the statement that "wealth has made me happier." Even more surprising was the discovery that 10 percent of millionaires (and 16 percent of women millionaires) felt that their wealth actually created *more* problems than it solved.

The American wealth boom has not only created more rich people; it has also created more rich-people problems. While money has showered Richistanis with obvious benefits, like freedom, power and all those boats and planes, it has also burdened them with troubles they never imagined on their climb to the top.

There are family squabbles, endless choices in how to

spend and invest their money and a constant fear of losing it all in the financial markets, à la Pete Musser. There are multiple homes to manage, staffs to oversee and a flood of new bills to pay, from plumbers and gardeners to art restorers and jewelry advisers. If Richistanis thought money would make their lives simpler, they were mistaken. It's made their lives far more complicated.

At the same time, Richistanis are frustrated by all the competition with all the other Richistanis. No matter how well they're doing, someone else is always doing better. As we saw in the first chapter, Richistanis feel they need *twice* their current fortunes to feel secure, no matter what their wealth. Those worth $1 million say they need $2 million, and those worth $10 million say they need $20 million.

In his book *The Virtue of Prosperity,* Dinesh D'Souza writes that today's rich "keep chasing one opportunity after another . . . they keep at it, hoping to become top dog, awaiting a tranquility that never arrives."

All that striving and worrying has made Richistanis an especially anxious elite. Yet rather than grappling privately with their problems, like the Old Money crowd, Richistanis have come up with a more novel solution—one that could exist only in an age of millions of millionaires.

They've formed their own wealth support groups.

On a recent Thursday morning, 10 middle-aged men gather at a Manhattan townhouse, formerly home to a German singing society. They're dressed casually, in khakis, button-down shirts, sweaters and Merrells. They sit around a large meeting table, munching on fruit and chatting about their kids, vacations and the weather. The atmosphere is relaxed and familiar, like breakfast buddies meeting up at the local diner. But to get into this break-fast, you have to be worth at least $10 million.

The meeting is part of Tiger 21, the nation's biggest "wealth peer group." A wealth peer group is a new kind of club where members of similar net worths get together to swap advice on everything from hedge funds and stocks to family and the personal effects of wealth. It's where the self-help culture meets the wealth boom. And it's become a thriving cottage industry.

This morning's Tiger meeting begins with the "Global Update," where each Tiger member talks about what's happening in his financial and personal life (Tiger is predominantly male). The first to unburden himself is Michael Sonnenfeldt, Tiger's founder and a former New York real-estate developer.

Sonnenfeldt has a problem. He and a good friend coinvested in a small company and they clashed over the business strategy. Now, the friendship is ruined and Sonnenfeldt's seven-figure investment is at risk.

"I've never lost a friendship over a deal," he says. "I never realized what a psychological toll this would take on me. I mean, it's really consumed my life. I'd say it's taking up maybe a third of my psychological and business energy. My choices are to stay involved in the business, because I have so much invested, or I could just get out. So now I'm just wondering what I should do. It's been really painful for me."

The group members nod their heads in sympathy. A few say he should resign from the board.

"Yeah, I think that's what I need to do," Sonnenfeldt says. "You're right, I need to disengage, I need to let it go."

Another member, a former media executive, says he's renovating his Manhattan co-op and, unlike most of the New York wealthy, he's decided not to move out during the construction. The mess, noise and disruption have become almost unbearable, he says.

"I've never been through anything like it," he says. "We've been thinking of finding a place that's bigger and better. This might be an impetus for us to get a new place."

The executive says his investments are doing fine, but "I'm also looking for more international equity exposure, if anyone has any ideas."

George, a retired entrepreneur from the Midwest, says he's worried about his local economy, which has suffered from a decline in manufacturing. Granted, his own finances are fine, since he makes about $1 million a year from serving on corporate boards. Yet being a community-minded person, George says he's nervous about the job losses, which seem to be trickling up to the owners of all the million-dollar homes going up for sale nearby.

"It's worrying to me to see all the uncertainty," he says.

Al, an energetic manufacturing and real-estate magnate, said he's struggling to close his factory without inflicting too much pain on his workers. "I've got a lot of volume and a lot of employees, and it's going to take a lot of time to get it sorted out," he says. "That's really been taking up a lot of my time and energy. It's very difficult."

On the bright side, he says his real-estate investments and international funds are doing great. He adds that he and his family are enjoying their newly renovated 6,000-square-foot vacation home on Long Island.

Arthur, a top executive at a financial services firm,

says he's torn over what to do with his large holdings of company stock. The share price had recently dropped, he said, and as long as he stays with the company, he can't hedge the position.

"So basically you're working to reduce your assets," Sonnenfeldt says.

Arthur frowns. "Well, I already sold three-quarters of my stock years ago."

"Fine," Sonnenfeldt says. "I'm just saying you could be in a sucker's bet."

Another member named Al, a tanned, portly, former Wall Street executive, is in particularly good spirits after celebrating his 77th birthday. He says he just had a physical and his cholesterol was down to 107 from 287, thanks to a combination of Lipitor and Zetia. The group applauds and everyone scribbles down the names of the two drugs.

On the financial side, Wall Street Al says he regrets selling more than half of the shares of his firm's stock years ago after his retirement to diversify. The stock soared in 2005 and today his holdings—if he hadn't sold—would have been worth more than $100 million.

"You were too close to the business," one of the members says.

"A lot of us make that mistake," says another. "Don't beat yourself up. It happens."

Adding to his remorse, Wall Street Al says his lifestyle is getting more expensive. To keep up his cash "burn rate," he says he has to start getting higher returns on his investments. He passes around brochures for two multimillion-dollar homes that he bought for speculation in Cape Cod and is now trying to sell.

"They're great properties," he says. "You can help me out."

He says he tried investing in several top-performing private-equity funds—investment pools that invest in private companies—but they were all closed, since they already had too much cash from investors. There are so many rich people trying to invest in private-equity funds, and able to meet the $5 million or $10 million minimum investments, that the funds are literally turning away investors.

"The good funds have too much cash," he said. "It's very frustrating; you can't get these guys to take your money. Everyone's rejecting me."

"Same thing happened to me," another member says.

"There's too much money in the system," Sonnenfeldt says.

Yet there's not nearly enough money in their bank accounts, the members complain. Later in the day, the talk turns to inflation. The costs of living the high life are soaring, they say, but their investment returns are starting to slow. In the late 1990s and early 2000s, returns were easily 10 percent or more. Now they're more like 5 percent to 7 percent, while inflation for the wealthy is rising in the double digits. To maintain their lifestyles, some of the Tiger members said they might have to start dipping into their principal—a violation of accepted wealth-planning rules.

"My wife buys these Manolo Blahniks and they keep going up in price," says Manufacturing Al. "I had to tell her to slow down because it was just getting absurd."

"Look at restaurant prices," says Wall Street Al. "It's $250 for two people now."

"Or courtside NBA tickets," says George. "They're $850

each. Okay, maybe the cushions on the chairs are more comfortable, but still. . . ."

"You don't even realize it, but your lifestyle expands," adds Manufacturing Al. "Or if you want a good Mercedes, they're now $100,000. Do I need to have one? No, but you want to have nice things because we earned it. We grow accustomed to a certain lifestyle and it's getting more expensive."

"And it's competitive," says Wall Street Al. "When you go to the Hamptons you want a nice house, but the guy next door has an even nicer house. And the price goes up each year, so you have to decide if you want that nicer house or if you want to go someplace else. It's also nice to fly on a private jet. But it gets expensive."

The media executive jumps in. "I'm surprised that any of us are really worried about this. Do you really think you're going to run out of money?"

"You don't live in my house," jokes Wall Street Al. "Compounding works both ways. It's that shrinkage that you worry about. I can't live on 5 percent or 6 percent return on my investments anymore. It's not good enough. I need more."

George adds, "In creating wealth, it's not just greed that motivates you, it's fear. There really is a lot of interconnection between fear and greed. And if people stay worried, it's part of what motivates them. We're always worried."

"You wonder how much is really enough," says another member. "How much do you think you need to have so you wouldn't worry? Ten years ago, I used to think $5 million was enough to stay above the water line. Now it's more. What's the number? Is it $10 million? $50 million?"

The group ponders the question. The media executive chuckles and says: "These are pretty high-class problems."

The Inner Millionaire

In 1998, Michael Sonnenfeldt retired from his real-estate business a wealthy man. He had sold his stake in his company for tens of millions of dollars and had millions more from the sale of a previous business. Yet he was troubled.

A towering man, with a white beard, a broad smile and a penchant for Nehru collars, the 51-year-old Sonnenfeldt likes to talk about "finding meaning" beyond wealth. He's a self-professed Jewish Buddhist who goes to meditation retreats in Montana and makes regular pilgrimages to Japan to "absorb the aesthetic." (He and Larry Ellison use the same Japanese interior designer.)

After selling his real-estate company, Sonnenfeldt felt a sudden emptiness in his soul. The business had been the center of his life. And now it was gone.

"My business was not only my main source of wealth, it was also a main source of my identity," he says. "The question was how to live my life without my business. It was about figuring out who I was without it."

There was also the more practical question of income. After cashing out of his real-estate company, Sonnenfeldt realized his earnings depended on his financial investments. Yet he knew little about the high-end investment world. For the rich, investing used to mean simple stocks and bonds. Now, it's all about commodity funds, private-equity funds, derivatives and currency swaps—things even

Sonnenfeldt, who worked at Goldman Sachs before getting into real estate, didn't fully understand.

"I had to learn how to be an investor and preserve my wealth," Sonnenfeldt says. "That's a very different world from real estate."

Sonnenfeldt started talking to friends who were in a similar situation. All of a sudden, there was a vast population of rich people who had sold their businesses and were searching for new identities and investment expertise. While Old Money used to rely on their trusted family attorneys and bankers, Richistanis no longer trust today's giant private banks and brokers, which are often more focused on pushing their own financial products than providing objective advice. The new breed of do-it-yourself rich people wanted to take control of their financial futures, just as they were taking control of their philanthropy.

Sonnenfeldt had been a member of a CEO group called The Executive Committee, where members swapped management ideas. After he retired, he invited several other members to help start a kind of "post-CEO" group.

Initially the idea was to focus on investments, like the Beardstown Ladies Investment Club, but for multimillionaires. Sonnenfeldt named the club Tiger 21, which stood for The Investment Group for Enhanced Results. (He added the "21" so it wouldn't be confused with Julian Robertson's former hedge fund, called Tiger.)

Tiger 21 now has 80 members, divided into subgroups of 10 or 12 people who meet every month. Each member pays $25,000 a year in dues (which can be tax deductible). Initially Sonnenfeldt set a wealth ceiling for members of

$100 million. But that quickly disappeared, since he got so many members who were far richer.

As for the $10 million minimum, Sonnenfeldt said research showed the population of decamillionaires was among the fastest-growing populations in the country. He also found that investors with more than $10 million behaved differently than those with less than $10 million.

"There's no magic number, but the $10 million people are investing to maximize their long-term wealth and below that number the investing is characterized by generating current returns for income."

As Tiger started to grow, a surprising thing started to happen. During the meetings, members started talking about the personal problems that stemmed from wealth. Like raising rich children. Or losing friendships. Or preventing family fights over money.

Getting together with a group of strangers who were equally rich proved oddly liberating. And in a world where the wealthy feel like constant targets, Tiger was like an intellectual gated community. They felt safe.

"I tell my group things I wouldn't even tell my husband or my kids," said one of Tiger's few female members. "These people know everything about me, from how much I spend on shoes to my feelings about my mother. I tell them everything."

At one meeting, a Tiger member confided that he was growing distant from his teenage daughter. He had devoted much of his life to his business and now that he was retired, he wanted to reconnect with his family. One of the other members suggested taking her out to breakfast every Saturday morning.

The father took the advice and at the next meeting,

he told the group that the weekly breakfasts had changed his life.

"His relationship with his daughter was transformed by these breakfasts," Sonnenfeldt recalls. "The father was crying, the guy who gave him the advice was crying, everyone in the room broke down. It was a really powerful moment."

At another meeting, a tech tycoon who retired young was searching for a new career. He tried music. He tried money management. He tried producing theater. Nothing made him happy. Tiger members reminded him how much he liked teaching children, so he started teaching troubled youths at a juvenile detention center. He loved the job, and it became his new calling.

"We sort of guided him to the answer that was there all along," said one member.

Growing from word of mouth, Tiger has become so popular that it is planning on opening other offices around the country, and perhaps in Europe.

Indeed, the idea of rich people helping rich people is gaining in popularity. CCC Alliance in Boston, another peer group, only accepts members worth $100 million or more, but it has more than 80 families as members. The group has also linked up with families in Europe.

MetCircle in New York has a minimum wealth level of $100 million, and it's just passed the 100-member mark. Other groups include $M3 in California, New York's Institute for Private Investors and the Family Office Exchange in Chicago. A group of New York–based women who have made their own fortunes, largely in finance, have banded together to form Circle Financial, the first all-female wealth peer group.

Laird Pendleton, CCC's founder and an heir to the Pitcairn family fortune, says the popularity of wealth peer groups speaks to the skeptical, independent spirit of today's rich.

"When you're wealthy, the world is always trying to sell you something, and families like mine value their privacy," he says. "Peer groups give you a group of families that you can get to know and trust over time. They've walked in your shoes and they may have even been down the same path. Rather than reinventing an issue, like generational transfers or bringing your in-laws into the family business, you can ask someone who's been through it, and get objective advice. What we hear over and over from our families is 'We don't want to reinvent the wheel.'"

Peer groups also offer members access to premium financial information and deals. They bring in top economists, private-equity deal makers, traders and hedge-fund managers to offer their insights into markets. The specialists are happy to spend the time, since peer groups are filled with potential clients.

Members also bring each other into their own deals. One peer, for instance, might know about a hotel going up in Shanghai that's looking for co-owners, or a start-up software company that suddenly needs capital. Over the past few years, Tiger members have teamed up to buy oil rigs, launch food companies and coinvest in investment funds. At CCC, some members opted to invest with a tech entrepreneur who returned to his native India to scout for business opportunities.

"One of the advantages to our network is that it's global," says Stephen Martiros, managing partner of CCC.

"And that's hugely important to today's wealth, which has a truly international perspective."

What the Rich Talk About When They Talk About Money

Late in the afternoon during the Tiger meeting, the members are gathered around the table for the day's main event—the portfolio defense. If the mission of Tiger 21 is to bare your soul (and finances) to your rich peers, the portfolio defense is the ultimate disrobing. At each meeting, a Tiger member reveals every detail of his personal balance sheet, from investments and income to charities and household spending. In analyzing someone's spending and income, the group winds up probing deeper questions like "what is your goal in life?" and "what fulfills you?" Sonnenfeldt calls it "carefrontation"—part intervention, part support group.

George is the day's subject. He hands out a five-page summary of his balance sheet and expense statements, showing a portfolio valued at around $50 million. Beyond his investments, which earn around $300,000 a year, he earns about $800,000 a year from serving on corporate boards. His spending rate varies from about $750,000 to $1.3 million a year, about half of which goes for taxes and charities, with the rest going for mortgage payments, restaurants, cars, a vacation home, family holidays and other daily costs.

He begins the defense by talking about his money managers.

"The people I have are good," he says. "But I still feel like I'm spending too much time on accounting and record keeping. I'm still the general contractor with my investments and I don't want to be."

His broader goal, he says, is to "create financial security and independence to allow me to spend more time raising my kids and have a more balanced life."

As he talks, the members begin to pore over the numbers.

Manufacturing Al notices that George owns a lot of stock in the companies where he also serves as a director—essentially doubling his risk if the companies fail.

"Aren't you doubly exposed here?" he says. "They might seem like very good investments last year but you never know."

George says he prefers to invest in the companies he directs, since he can have more control over his investments. He also feels that investing makes him a better director, since he has "skin in the game."

"When I am (financially) involved in a situation, I get very aggressive," George says. "Maybe that's not a good thing."

The group then homes in on what they all see as George's weakness. His portfolio is 60 percent bonds and 40 percent stocks, far too conservative for someone of George's relatively young age (he's in his early 50s).

"I would question why you're just treading water here," another member says. "You're a smart guy, you're plugged into a lot of opportunities, I would be going for more growth."

"You're still young, you're still earning a nice income from boards every year, you can afford to be more aggressive," says Wall Street Al. "At this stage in your life you should be taking more risk and get a higher return. You can get a lot more out of your portfolio."

Arthur suggests international equities, and Wall Street Al suggests a money manager.

"I think you might even have an inflation risk here," Arthur says, adding that George's rising living costs could leave him scraping for cash in a decade or so. "You may not, but I don't think you want to take that chance. You don't want it to bite you in the behind 20 years from now. One thing you could do is take the money out of bonds and put it into something with higher returns."

George says, "You're right; my lifestyle is expanding. When my wife and I went through this exercise to figure out our costs, she was in shock. Our lifestyle was growing and we didn't really realize it."

On the personal front, George says he's nervous about the impact of his wealth on his kids. He said his oldest son had taken control of his trust and had earned 20 percent on investments.

"That was really encouraging," George says.

But he says he's not sure about the impact of money on his other two kids. And he's already having trouble figuring out how to split up their beach home if and when he leaves it to his children.

"That could be a disaster," one member says.

"All three will be fighting over it," says another.

George says he hopes one of them will be successful enough to buy out the others.

Wall Street Al has another solution: George can buy his two Cape Cod homes, "then all three kids will be happy." George says, "See, at Tiger, we solve each other's problems."

———

BEYOND worrying about money, Richistanis also worry about their kids. Their fears can be boiled down to two words: Paris Hilton.

Richistanis want to give their children luxuries that they never enjoyed growing up. Yet they also want them to have a strong work ethic, which can only come from struggle. To help reconcile these two urges, and teach the next generation how to handle all that money, Richistanis are turning to a new kind of summer camp.

11

ARISTOKIDS*

We'll Always Have Paris

Ryan Achterberg, a 23-year-old Californian, is sitting across the table from his fiancée.

"There's something we need to talk about," she tells Ryan. "I'm so excited about our wedding and being with you the rest of my life. But I need to ask you something."

"Of course," Ryan says. "I'm here for you."

"My family would like us to sign a marital agreement."

"You mean a prenup?"

"Well, in my family we like to call it a marital agreement."

---

*Some of the following names have been changed to protect the identities of the kids and their families.

"You don't trust me? I'm committing my life to you. I thought I was a part of your family."

"You know I trust you," she says.

"But not enough to let me into your family."

"This is not about our relationship," she says. "What should happen if I died and you wanted to remarry? You can understand my family would want to protect their assets."

Ryan shakes his head. "I am not having this conversation."

Fortunately for Ryan, he and his fiancée aren't actually engaged. His "fiancée" is Dr. Lee Hausner, a psychologist who's become one of the country's top advisers to the children of the new rich. And their mock conversation, where wealthy Ryan played the part of the poor, pre-nupped suitor, was part of a two-day course run by Hausner called the "Financial Life Skills Retreat."

The Skills Retreat is a new kind of summer camp for young Richistanis. For two days in July, and another two days in October, the sons and daughters of today's multi-millionaires and billionaires gather in a classroom at the University of California–Irvine to learn how to manage the vast fortunes they're about to inherit. They talk about portfolio theory, price-to-earnings ratios and debt management. They learn how to convince their intended to sign prenups and how to ask their dads for loans. They learn basic "life skills," like how to control their spending, how to work with others and how to interview for a job. Most of all, they learn how *not* to squander their fortunes.

Turning a group of privileged Southern California youths into savvy investors and professionals represents a triumph of hope over history. Yet it's a hope that IFF Advisors, the company that runs the Skills Retreat, finds increasingly common among today's Richistanis who are about to entrust their children with millions.

"There's this massive wealth transfer that's about to happen, and that's already occurring, and yet the kids who are receiving it are not ready," says Doug Freeman, IFF's president. "That's going to be a problem."

Aristokids

The American wealth boom has created a boomlet of rich kids, and a new generation of anxious Richistani parents. Based on average family size, there are now more than four million children of American millionaires. And all those silver spoons are dipping into a record amount of disposable income and inherited wealth.

Up to $15 trillion will be passed down to the children of millionaires between 2002 and 2052, according to a study by the Boston College Social Welfare Institute. Much of that will be passed down from baby boomers (and even younger parents) to their kids. While economists differ on the exact amounts that will be passed down, few doubt that the wealth boom of the past decade will create a cascade of cash flowing to the next generation.

A survey by Prince & Associates, a wealth research firm, found that most millionaires today plan to leave at least 75 percent of their estates to their children. The number is highest for families with households worth $25 million or more, disproving the widely held notion that wealthier families are more likely to leave a greater share to charity.

Today's rich are also indulging their kids. With little

time and plenty of disposable income, nearly 40 percent of today's millionaires give their kids unregulated access to the kids' own money. All that spending has helped create a new economy built around a new set of kiddie elites.

High-end resorts are building five-star kids' centers and playgrounds. When Ellen Perry, a wealth-education expert and mom, went to the Four Seasons in Scottsdale, Arizona, the staff greeted her four-year-old daughter with a child's bathrobe and a platter holding a freshly baked cookie with her named inscribed with icing. Each day at 4 P.M., the staff delivered coconut Popsicles and smoothies to the children's pool, and the resort's restaurants had child-sized silver flatware.

The Breakers Hotel in Palm Beach, once a bastion of blue-blood wealth and retirees, has become a giant rich-kid playground. The pool is packed on Sunday mornings with 30-something moms balancing mimosas and toddlers, and the hotel has built a giant family entertainment complex, with a kid-friendly Italian restaurant, craft and computer rooms, a toddler play area and babysitters.

Down the street, a children's clothing shop called Aristokids is doing a brisk business in $175 sandals and Juicy Couture miniskirts for preteens. Jodi Wentley, one of the owners, told me that one of the store's fastest-selling items is a pair of crocodile-skin Sperry topsiders, with deerskin lining and gold eyelets. The price: $899 a pair.

"They look great on a yacht," he says.

Private schools are now inundated with applicants, even as tuition for kindergarten soars to $27,000 at the top schools. In some cities, there are at least three private-school applicants for each available space. Television is filled with images of young wealth gone wild, with pouty heiresses demanding new Mercedes and $200,000 birthday parties. Paris Hilton kicked off the trend with *The Simple Life*, a reality show where the doe-eyed sex symbol slums it on an Arkansas farm. MTV's *Rich Girls* chronicled the shopping expeditions of Tommy Hilfiger's teenage daughter, Ally, and her friend, Jaime Gleicher, while the channel's other teen-spending fantasy, *My Super Sweet 16*, shows the sons and daughters (mostly daughters) of the newly rich vying for the title of most profligate birthday party.

All that extravagance has created new parenting problems—and new industries to solve them. A spate of recent research studies is shedding more light on how wealth, in addition to giving kids advantages, can become a family curse. Without the need to work, children develop little sense of motivation or drive. They have trouble developing basic life skills—cleaning up, managing money, working with other people—since they're used to relying on house staff and parents.

"When you have someone there to do virtually every chore, that really changes the life of a kid," says Ellen Perry, the Wealthbridge founder. "You don't learn basic skills that are fundamental building blocks for the rest of your life. The privilege gets in the way of healthy maturation. Money gives people the ability to buy their way out of life experiences. The parents may think they're helping their child, but they're actually robbing them."

Other side effects are more serious. Research by Suniya Luthar, a professor of psychology and education at the Teachers College of Columbia University, finds that today's affluent kids are just as prone to substance abuse and "rule-breaking" behavior as inner-city kids. While the most common delinquencies among inner-city kids involve weapons and fights, affluent kids are prone to stealing from parents and friends.

Luthar also found that one in five affluent kids is clinically depressed—far more than the national norm. A study of private schools found that alcohol and drug use among affluent kids is even *higher* than that of inner-city kids. One reason the rates are comparable: absent parents. Wealthy kids today are often raised by a revolving door of nannies and house staff and see little of their parents.

"They tend to be more isolated from their parents physically and emotionally," Luthar says. Yet she added that the pressures to succeed for affluent kids also play a huge role.

Today's mini-Richistanis are surrounded by so many other Richitanis—a function of their population growth—that they've become insulated from the rest of society. They're growing up in a bubble of opulence. And they have little understanding that another world (in fact, most of the world) exists outside of their $17,000 Victorian custom playhouses and $25,000-a-year private schools. A private banker in New York told me the story of the 11-year-old daughter of a real-estate magnate who grew up flying on the family's private jet. For her birthday, the girl asked her father for a ride on a commercial flight.

"But we have our own jet," the magnate told her.

"I know, but I want to ride on a big plane with other people," she said. "I want to see what an airport looks like on the inside."

Lori Stoll, who lives in a Mediterranean mansion in Palm Beach, gets constant requests from her three kids to buy electronic gadgets and toys that other kids have at the Palm Beach Day School.

"They come home and say, 'So and so got an Xbox 360 and a go-cart and a pinball machine yesterday.' I say, 'That's nice. But you can't have it just because you're deserving of it. You have to wait for your birthday or holiday time for that to happen.' "

Richistanis stand in stark contrast to Old Money when it comes to parenting. Before the 1980s, inherited wealth was largely confined to blue-blood families that had time-honored traditions of raising rich kids. They rarely talked about money. They taught their children the importance of keeping a low profile, never embarrassing the family and choosing careers that were respectable without being mercenary. They instilled the notion the rich were different, with greater freedoms and greater responsibilities to society. And they relied on time-honored institutions—boarding schools, summer camps, churches, clubs, the Ivy League—to mold their offspring into a well-mannered elite. (Not that it always worked.)

Nelson Aldrich Jr., a Rockefeller cousin and author of *Old Money,* says boarding school played a particularly important role among the pre-Richistani crowd.

"When I grew up, the ethical tradition was this weird combination of Christianity and manliness. There was a heavy emphasis on sports, especially the most painful sports, like ice hockey and football. It was all about stoicism and patience under great stress. Boarding school was not what it is today, this kind of country club atmosphere. It was almost totalitarian. What they were saying was that in order for you to lead the good life you have to forget about all this money and this luxury and this freedom that you are heir to."

His family stressed the importance of adversity—even

if those adversities had to be manufactured. Aldrich, for instance, had a string of blue-collar summer jobs, including working at a boatyard, digging trenches in the Tetons for a rural electrification project, and working in the morgue of a local hospital.

"After the morgue job, my status among my friends went zipping straight up," he says.

Old Money wanted their kids to be productive, but not *too* productive. They wanted them to be free of worldly concerns to focus on higher aspirations, like art, culture or philanthropy. In his documentary *Born Rich,* Jamie Johnson, an heir to the Johnson & Johnson fortune, asks his father what he should do with his life now that he was turning 21. His father, also a trust-fund kid who never had to work, tells Jamie to join a charitable organization and give some of his money away. When Jamie rejects the ideas, his father looks puzzled and suggests finding a hobby, "like collecting old maps."

Old Money also handed over the family fortune to their kids with little or no instruction.

"The tradition when I was growing up was that you went to a meeting at the law firm of Choate Hall & Stewart in Boston and the family lawyer would explain the terms of the trust that you were going to live on for the rest of your life and that was it," Aldrich says. "There was no education. You took the backseat to your advisers and trust experts. It was just madness. We had zero training."

Richistanis don't want to repeat the mistakes of Old Money, which, they say, bred ignorance and indolence. Boarding schools are out; day schools are in. Most Richistanis rose up from the middle class and place great importance on passing on the work ethic to their kids—even as they indulge them with luxuries. In one study, 86 percent of wealthy parents say it's important for their kids to "learn the value of money through hard work." Yet only one-third encourage their kids to take after-school jobs.

Richistanis want their kids to be strivers. They want them to make money. Or at the very least, not to lose it.

The result is a booming new industry in wealth education for rich kids. Rather than leaving their financial fates in the hands of lawyers and bankers, Richistanis are sending their kids to special programs to become smarter stewards of the family cash.

At the Washington, D.C.–based Wealthbridge Partners, which caters to families worth $100 million or more, kids as young as seven spend a night at a zoo to study how it works as a business. Older kids help launch businesses, like greeting-card companies and lemonade stands. At the Wealthbridge lemonade stands, kids create "production teams" to run a cost-benefit analysis of using real lemons versus ready-made powder. They appoint "capital budget groups" to keep an eye on costs. And they form "location assessment units" to scout grocery stores, street corners and malls and look for the best place to set up shop. To demonstrate their budding noblesse oblige, the kids donate all their profits to charity.

IFF, the other big educator, has so much demand for its programs that it's opening offices in Dallas, New York and southern Florida to add to its California headquarters. It's biggest problem is finding qualified teachers for all the wealthy kids who need training. IFF charges between $5,000 and $15,000 for its various programs, which include one-day workshops for a single family to weekend courses for 15 or 20 kids at a time.

Increasingly, parents are also sending their kids to IFF and others for character training. As part of its financial course, IFF also tries to teach leadership skills, confidence building, negotiating skills and basic communication.

Says Freeman: "We're not trying to change the parenting. We're trying to teach the core values like responsibility, accountability, integrity that most families want to teach. But not all of them do it well. They haven't lived that lifestyle and maybe the modeling isn't that good."

Indeed, a two-day IFF workshop shows that today's wealth-education camps can go only so far to turn today's rich kids into street-smart investors.

The Sums of Our Fathers

At 7:30 A.M. at the University of California–Irvine campus, a stream of Land Rovers, BMWs and Mercedes pulls into a parking lot. A collection of tired-looking 20-somethings shuffle out of their cars, file into a classroom and introduce themselves over Diet Cokes and donuts.

Among the first to arrive is Kyle Circle, a spiky-haired entrepreneur in jeans and a T-shirt, who mentions that his father is California's strawberry king. Tina and Lisa, platinum-blond sisters, say their grandfather made a fortune in real estate. A tall, earnest young man named Tim, wearing a green polo shirt and khakis, says his dad owns a farm in Minnesota ("it's a pretty big farm," he admits). A brother and sister whose dad made a fortune from stationery, take their seats in the back of the room and look impatiently at their watches. This being California, the room fills with several real-estate scions, including Ryan.

Several other attendees belong to a family that made its money from an electrical contracting business that was sold. Rounding out the group are Kelsey and Kara, willowy brunettes whose family runs a garbage-hauling empire. All together the kids in the room represent family wealth of more than $3 billion.

To start out, the kids are asked why they decided to come to the class.

"My dad kind of suggested that I come," said a developer's daughter. "Actually, he more than suggested. He said it was kind of a requirement for my inheritance."

Tina says: "My grandmother said if I did this, she'd give me money to go to Vegas."

Hausner gets things rolling with a lesson on families and money. After spending 19 years as the senior psychologist in the Beverly Hills school system, Hausner is an expert on talking to rich kids, especially about family problems. With her broad smile, frosted hair and pastel-colored business suits, she's the model of a cheery, supportive West Coast therapist.

The class is divided into groups and told to answer a series of questions.

"How important is money to you today?"

One group answers: "Really important."

"It's important but it's not who we are," says another group.

"Very important for, like, survival," says another.

"To live," says another group. "You need it to live."

Hausner asks a follow-up: "How was money used in your family?"

"Educations, vacations, and a way to get control."

"Rewards."

"Investments and charity."

"To buy love," says one group. "Like Disneyland dads, where they confuse money and love."

"Very good," Hausner says. "Did you hear that? Disneyland dad. That's a very important concept. I want you to get in touch with that."

She moves on to the next question. "What do you remember your father saying about money?"

"Nothing is free," says one student.

"Don't be complacent," says another.

"Money doesn't grow on trees," says one.

"Trash is cash," say the waste-management heiresses.

Hausner asks about the dangers of money.

"Drugs," says one group.

"You become lazy. You don't want to work because you don't have to."

"Other people's perceptions. If they know you come from money, they think you're spoiled. The whole silver spoon thing."

"Or if you're dating, you're always worried about someone taking advantage of you. And on dates you have to, like, pay for things all the time. You're worried that they like you for your money."

"People come out of the woodwork to be your friend," Kyle says.

Hausner closes the session with one final question: What would the students do if they won the lottery?

"How much is the prize?" says Kyle.

"Let's say $10 million," Hausner says.

"Is that after-tax or pretax," says Ryan. "Because that's not that much pretax."

"Either way, it's not that much," Kyle says.

"Probably just invest it," the group says.

Tina mutters: "I'd go to Vegas."

Hausner leads to another lesson on prenups. When it comes to talking to a spouse-to-be about a prenup, Hausner has some basic rules. First, she says, don't wait until the month before the wedding to bring it up with your intended.

"Talk to them about it as soon as you know the relationship is serious," she says. "The closer you get to the wedding, the worse it's going to get. You should take them aside, maybe over dinner or at home, and say 'There's something important I need to share with you. In my family we do prenups.'"

Her second rule: Blame it on the family. If the future spouse pushes back, you can always say it's a family tradition or Dad's requirement. And make sure to call it a "marital agreement," instead of "prenup."

"This is like a business contract," Hausner says. "Tell the person that the money that you bring to the marriage is like a gift, that you didn't make it, but that the two of you can enjoy it during your marriage. You can say that your parents believe it's important to execute a prenup so more of the money will stay in the bloodline."

When all else fails in selling a prenup, Hausner says, it's better to talk about death than divorce.

"You also say 'Well, what if I got run over by a bus and you remarried? It wouldn't be fair for my family's money to pass to your new spouse.' Or you can turn it around to talk about the future for your own kids. You can say, 'Well, if we had children, you would want the same thing for them, wouldn't you? If we had a daughter and she got married you would want the same protection for her, wouldn't you? You would want to keep the money in the family.'"

The class nods attentively. Two students who were just married to each other offer to share their story. The husband, Keith, didn't come from money and works as a schoolteacher. He dated Sarah, the daughter of a California real-estate developer, for months before learning that her family had money.

"We were sitting in the car, driving to her dad's house," Keith says. "And she says "Oh, by the way, my family is pretty well-off.' And I said 'Okay.' I was picturing maybe a decent, two-story house. We get to Malibu and we pull up to these gates and there's this huge, five-story house with all these wings. We take a tour of the house, and I said 'Okay, well, this is more than just well-off.' There are still parts of the house I've never seen and I've done several tours."

Before their wedding, his fiancée asked Keith to sign a marital agreement.

"When I first heard about it, it sounded pretty strange. But I sat down with this attorney and he basically explained the idea of community property. Everything she brings to the marriage is hers, everything I bring in is mine, and anything we make together is community property. It sounded pretty fair to me."

As the day goes on, the kids in the IFF class start to talk openly about their lives and money. Some have turned into drifters and spenders, others are hard-driven professionals and entrepreneurs. Few want to follow their parents' footsteps—either in business or life.

Tim, the farmer's son, works in IT at a big company in

Minnesota. Two of the students are artists, two are teachers and one woman is a chef. Tina and Lisa, who have already blown the first installment of their inheritence, are starting their own beauty salons.

Kelsey and Kara, who live in Malibu, are still searching for careers. Kelsey writes songs part-time and is looking to break into the music business. Kara, who's still in college, is a top competitor in the show-horse circuit. Like many Richistani offspring, the sisters have an ambivalent view of wealth.

Growing up in Southern California, they had all the comforts of a wealthy family. Kara drove a Mercedes to high school. They had nice clothes. When she was eight, she got her first horse and now she has about 45.

The sisters don't "act" like rich girls and have the laid-back, down-to-earth air of regular college kids. Yet having friends of lesser wealth has proven complicated. One recent winter, they invited a friend to join them in Hawaii, where the sisters had vacationed for years. They always got a suite at the Grand Wailea, but to accommodate their friend, they got a smaller room on the ground floor.

"It was this tiny room, in this weird part of the hotel we'd never even seen before," Kara says. "We stayed there for a night, but the room was so bad we just couldn't deal, so we had to upgrade. We paid for everything in the end because we didn't want our friend to have to pay. I'm not sure we'd do that again. It was awkward."

Watching their parents work 14-hour days—their mom is the general manager of the company—the sisters gained a strong appreciation for hard work. Yet they also know they don't want their parents' workaholic lives—and they don't want to run the family business, at least not yet.

"I would like to do something on my own and make my own impact first," Kara says.

On the other hand, they're also growing tired of the hedonistic culture of Malibu, which they say is filled with young heirs and heiresses spending money and passing the time.

"It's so materialistic," Kara says. "It's all these people strung out on drugs and drifting from one thing to the next. It's not normal. I want to live in a normal place and have a normal life."

Kyle Circle marks the other extreme—the rich kid whose single obsession is to outdo his father.

At 21, he's launched two companies and hatched plans for several more. He works 16-hour days, drives the same used Ford pickup he bought in high school and saves half of his meager income in hopes of buying a house with his wife.

Circle's father is worth an estimated $300 million to $500 million, after building a strawberry-growing empire and selling out to a competitor. Kyle's grandfather also attained a level of fame in California produce circles: He created the baby carrot. Yet Kyle hasn't asked his family for money since he left home at age 19.

"The thing that keeps me going is wanting to have the same success as my dad," he says. "I don't want him handing it to me. I want to do it completely on my own. It's something I have to prove."

For now, he's just making ends meet. His music management company has yet to break into the big time. His other company, which sells wireless credit-card readers, generates income, but not much.

Still, Kyle knows from watching his dad that failure is a precondition to success. And he's not counting on any inheritance, even though he'll probably get one.

"I'm living my life assuming I won't receive a single penny. I don't know what type of money, if any, I'll get. Whatever I get, I have to earn."

Growing up, Kyle's family lived the life of striving middle classers. He did chores, but got no allowance. At age 11, he started buying strawberries from his dad (no discount) and sold them door-to-door in his neighborhood. Later he started buying melons and corn and sold them from a street corner every Saturday. Kyle's rich friends got whatever they wanted just for the asking. Yet when he asked his parents for a bike or basketball hoop, they would tell him to save and buy it himself.

"That kind of pissed me off," he says. "I remember being pretty upset at the time."

In high school he finally convinced his dad to give him a summer job at the company. But it wasn't the cushy office work he hoped for.

"He dropped me off in the field at 4 A.M. and told me to wait for the foreman to pick me up. I worked five days a week for minimum wage, picking and driving the tractor. I was the only white person there and I didn't speak Spanish. Nobody knew I was the owner's kid and I made sure they didn't find out, because then they would hate me. I ate off the lunch truck with everyone else. Man, it was terrible."

After that, Kyle swore he'd never work in produce.

Kyle suffered another defeat after high school, when he got rejected from the college of his choice, Chapman University. His grades were good, but his SAT scores fell short. Instead, he followed in the footsteps of his father, who skipped college to go into business.

As hard as he works, and as little as he makes, Kyle feels even more sorry for his rich friends from high school.

"I feel bad for them," he says. "They're still living at home. One guy I know does errands for his father—like dry cleaning and stuff—and gets $50,000 a year and he thinks it's a job. They just assume the money will always be there. They're spending it and they don't know what they're going to do when it's all gone. They don't have any skills, but they have really high standards like for sports cars and hotels. I guess I feel pretty lucky that my parents made it tough for me."

Trading Places

After lunch, the class divides into groups and receives a set of laptop computers for a stock-trading contest. Each group is given $100 in fictitious cash to spend and a list of stocks to choose from. The laptops run a trading program that simulates stock-market activity over a five-year period. When the clock starts, the students scream with excitement.

"Buy Toys "R" Us, I like that place," one of them says.

"What do we want this P-E thing to do?" says another.

"Oh, get Toyota, my dad just got my sister one."

"Apple is a good one. With iPods and all that."

At one point Tina interjects: "This is just gambling. You're better off going to Vegas."

The quietest group is Team 1, led by Tim, the farmer's son. With the rest of the group looking in, Tim goes through the stock list and methodically picks stocks with the highest margin of safety—a value-investor tool that measures the difference between the intrinsic value of a company and its stock price.

By the end of the competition, Tim's team is announced as the winner.

"It was pretty simple," he says. "I just focused on low PE and high margin of safety and ignored everything else."

The rest of the class stares at him blankly. Later one of them asks Tina a question: "So is a stock the same thing as a mutual fund?"

Most of the group looks stumped.

THAT night, the students attend a special dinner. They gather at the University Club, overlooking the campus lawns, and dig into plates of roasted chicken and grilled vegetables.

The night's speaker is Charles "Chuck" Martin, a top venture capitalist in Southern California and something of a cult hero among the Orange County business set. Martin, wearing an open-collared shirt, is a calm, soft-spoken man with a weathered face and a bright smile. He spends the next hour telling the group his inspiring rags-to-riches life story—the poor family in rural Ohio, the dad who worked at the post office, the first paper route.

"I never felt deprived," he said. "It was one of the great advantages. I never had anyone help me along. It was all up to me."

He worked two jobs in college and got three degrees.

"I had no social life," he says. "I went on two dates the entire time I was in college. For the first date, I took a girl out to have coffee. Thank God it was just coffee because I wouldn't have known what to do if it was anything more."

After college, Martin went to work for Hughes Electronics in California, working on missile systems. He later left with a senior manager to start a venture-capital firm, despite knowing little about the business.

"One of the fundamental requirements of being an entrepreneur is being naïve," he says.

Martin made most of his fortune investing in start-ups and leveraged buyouts. For 25 years, he co-owned the TEC Organization—a San Diego–based chief executives group that he later sold to Michael Milken and Larry Ellison for millions.

At the end of his talk, one of the real-estate heiresses asks a question.

"Do you have kids?" she asks.

"No, we don't," he says. "We are surrounded by kids, with nieces and nephews and everything. I have set aside money for scholarships for them, but that's it. We decided there would be no inheritance."

The students look puzzled. One whispers, "No inheritance? None?"

After they leave, I ask Chuck why he decided not to leave any money to his family.

"The nice thing about wealth is it's very empowering," he says. "But I think it can also have negative effects on people, especially with kids. One thing I was going to tell them, but I guess I decided not to, was that inherited money can be very damaging."

"These kids are at a real disadvantage in some ways." Martin stares out the window and watches the IFF students climb into their Mercedes and Land Rovers. "I almost feel sorry for them."

12

THE WEALTH GAP
AND THE FUTURE
OF RICHISTAN

In the fall of 2005, I flew to Ft. Lauderdale for the 46th Annual International Boat Show—the weeklong celebration of boats, beaches and billionaires. The boat show had become one of my yearly routines as *The Journal*'s wealth reporter; it was there, in 2004, that I met a Texas yachter who remarked that the American rich seemed to be floating off to their own country, giving rise to the notion of Richistan.

During the 2005 show, however, I learned a more sobering lesson.

Driving from the airport, I saw a city crippled by storms. Hurricane Wilma had pounded the region 10 days earlier, and Ft. Lauderdale's streets were still covered with broken glass, tree limbs and garbage. Most of the area's homes were still without power. Shops, restaurants and hotels were boarded up and the only people who seemed to be working were utility crews and Red Cross teams.

Wilma received scant attention from the media or government, since it followed just a month after the even greater tragedy of Katrina in New Orleans. Yet like Katrina, Wilma didn't just inflict physical damage. It also laid bare a vast social underclass.

Thousands of residents in the poorer sections of Ft. Lauderdale (most of them black or Hispanic) were left homeless. Many were herded into school gyms and classrooms because of the lack of affordable rental apartments. A small number of vouchers handed out by the Federal Emergency Management Agency were virtually useless, since they were well below local rental rates. While South Florida's overinflated housing market had been a boon to the wealthy, creating towers of million-dollar beach condos, it had wiped out most of the affordable housing.

"Virtually none of the (new) housing is for low or moderate income people," wrote the *Miami Herald.*

Pertrenia Craig, a mother of six, was shipped with her kids to two homeless shelters the week I was there.

"I'm about to cry right now," she told the local paper. "Am I supposed to sit in this shelter until they kick me out with my kids?"

Just a few miles away, the yacht show was kicking off its opening-day festivities. The Bahia Mar Marina was packed with gleaming, multimillion-dollar boats, their chrome rails and mahogany decks getting a fresh new polish from uniformed crews. Brokers were leading rich clients through the hushed staterooms and crystal-filled dining areas of the megayachts for sale, many priced at $20 million and up.

Many residents in Ft. Lauderdale were sweating through the tropical heat, without electricity. The yachts and vendor pavilions were perfectly chilled. At lunchtime, I walked into an air-conditioned hospitality tent provided by *Yacht Magazine,* where ultrawealthy buyers could come in from the heat. The guests sipped champagne, ate crab cakes and dipped strawberries into a giant chocolate fountain staffed by two leggy, blond waitresses. On the lawn outside, a local Rolls-Royce dealer was demonstrating the virtues of the new $340,000 Rolls-Royce Phantom.

"I just bought a Bentley last week," said a yacht owner from New Orleans who had ridden out the hurricane on his boat. "Terrific car. I can't wait for delivery."

Granted, a few yacht builders boycotted the show, saying it was inappropriate.

"We felt badly to go in there and have this show that celebrates luxury yachting, when residents of South Florida are still without a lot of basic necessities," said David Ross, the CEO of Burger Boat Co.

Yet the local mayor and the show's promoter, Kaye Pearson, insisted that the spending by the rich would help lift the town's spirits and economy. They denied that any local resources—police, electrical crews, phone repair men—had been diverted to the show. Still, Pearson promised that guests coming to buy a yacht would hardly know there had been a hurricane.

"You could come here and not notice any difference," said Pearson, proudly.

The dual realities in Ft. Lauderdale on that November day—the yachts, champagne bubbles and Rolls-Royces on one side of the city, and the homeless, destitute moms on the other—revealed an uncomfortable truth about Richistan. Even as Richistanis have exploded in number and wealth over the past decade, much of America is being left behind.

Median incomes for American households fell in 2005 for the fifth year in a row, and the median families are now making $3,000 less than they did in 2000, adjusted for inflation. Meantime, incomes for the richest are growing in the double digits.

By almost any measure, America is becoming a more unequal society. The richest 1 percent of Americans control more than 33 percent of the total wealth, and their wealth is now greater than the bottom 90 percent of Americans. The share of national income held by the top 1 percent of earners is now the highest since World War II.

Many of the core institutions in our society—education, politics, the health-care system—are becoming increasingly segregated by wealth. Tuition for top colleges is soaring, even as some of the grants for poorer students and state support for public universities have failed to keep pace. The rich, frustrated by the ineffectiveness of the health-care system, are increasingly turning to "concierge doctors" (the top specialists paid princely sums to serve a limited number of families) and abandoning the national health-care system. As political campaigns become more expensive, the rich have become increasingly important as sources of funding, thereby getting an outsized voice in policy.

Voter apathy, says James Lardner, founder of Inequality .Org, "flows from the suspicion of many Americans that meaningful political representation, like regular doctor's visits and four-year college, has been priced out of reach."

The gap between the rich and everyone else has imposed other costs. As we saw in the "Size Matters" chapter, the record consumption by the rich has set a new standard for the rest of the country to try to follow and left the middle class working harder and taking in more debt to keep up.

It has also, according to economist Robert H. Frank, made the rest of America less happy, since happiness is defined in large part by how well you're doing compared to those around you. With so many people getting so rich—and parading their riches on TV and in public—the nonrich feel increasingly envious, inadequate or a combination of the two. As a result, Americans are spending more of their incomes on unnecessary luxuries to prove their status, even as the country underfunds pressing problems like the public-school system, roads, bridges, health care or the environment. Frank writes, "As incomes continue to grow at the top and stagnate elsewhere, we will see even more of our national income devoted to luxury goods, the main effect of which will be to raise the bar that counts as luxury."

As I left the Ft. Lauderdale boat show in November, I started to wonder about these inequities. How much was *too* much? How long could Richistan last? Would the gap between Richistanis and the rest of America create a new wave of social and political unrest, as in the

Gilded Age and Roaring Twenties? Or would these gaps be tolerated as the inevitable consequence of global, high-tech capitalism?

The Gilded Age and Roaring Twenties both spawned voter backlashes, with Theodore Roosevelt busting the corporate trusts in the early 1900s and Franklin Delano Roosevelt ushering in the New Deal in the 1930s. Today, there's growing evidence that the Third Wave is also spawning voter frustration. With the middle and lower classes seeing less and less of the economic gains over the past decade, the resurgent Democrats are turning their attention to increasing the minimum wage, limiting global trade and trying to boost government funding for education.

Others are targeting the rich, mainly by raising their taxes. While conservatives argue that "Robin Hood" policies will choke off economic growth and reduce entrepreneurial incentives, some academics and policy experts say rebalancing the tax system is critical to a broad-based economy. Edward Wolff, the wealth expert at New York University, has proposed a special "wealth tax" on the richest households (the rates would vary by wealth levels).

"The only way to get more money to the middle class is to redistribute more money from the wealthy," Wolff says. "I think the tax system needs to be revamped, which will slow the growth among those at the very top."

The Democratic sweep of Congress in 2006 heralds a new wave of populist sentiment, driven in large part by middle-class discontent. Yet Americans aren't likely to reach for the pitchforks anytime soon. As morally troubling and politically charged as the issue of inequality has become, it's not likely to cause a populist revolt. Most

Americans still have a generally positive view of the wealthy and, rightly or wrongly, believe they too can make it to Richistan someday. Their preferred solution to inequality, according to polls, is to better nourish the middle class, rather than eating the rich.

"The focus for voters is on raising the living standards of the middle class, not on penalizing the top 1 percent," says Stan Greenberg, a Democratic pollster. "Their priority isn't to stop the top 1 percent from doing well."

Inequality, in short, isn't likely to shut down Richistan. If anything, the forces that have fueled Richistan's growth—the rising river of money from around the world, increasingly global markets and new technologies—remain strong. Experts predict that the number of millionaires and billionaires is likely to grow at least 6 percent a year in the coming years. In fact, as Richistan grows, inequality is likely to widen—not only between Richistan and America, but also between Lower and Upper Richistanis.

The Movable Feast

As we learned in the Third Wave chapter, Richistan owes its success largely to the giant river of money flowing around the world searching for good investments. The river has carried millions of Americans to Richistan, as it coursed into the stock market and other financial markets and lifted the fortunes of Instapreneurs, executives and stockholders. Americans could move more easily to Richistan in large part because money could move more easily around the world.

Throughout the 1990s, the river moved mainly to the United States. Our rapid economic growth, technological innovation, giant stock market, efficient financial system and relatively transparent business climate made it a logical place for both American and foreign investors to put their money.

Now, the river is expanding and spilling into other countries where the growth is stronger—mainly China, India and parts of Southeast Asia, eastern Europe and Latin America. As a result, Richistan is becoming more international. America will still be a huge engine of wealth creation, perhaps even more so as American companies and investors benefit from growth overseas. Yet over the next 5 to 10 years, production of millionaires will drift away from the United States.

Stephen Martiros, the managing director of CCC Alliance, the Boston-based peer group for the rich, likens Richistan to a "movable feast."

"What's created so much wealth in the United States is the rapid movement of capital from one part of the market and the world to another," he said. "For the last 10 years, the United States has been the safe haven for capital. We were the high ground. That will still be the case for some time. But the capital is also moving elsewhere, to Hong Kong, London, Singapore, Dubai."

These global shifts will effect Richistan in two big ways: It will become more globally diverse, and it will become more unequal.

As they become increasingly wealthy, the world's rich will form a "third" culture—not from their own country, or from America, but from a different, shared world of wealth. They'll stay at the same hotels (Four Seasons, Ritz

Carltons) drive the same cars (Bentleys, Rolls), eat many of the same foods (sushi fusion), wear the same clothes and accessories (Gucci, Vuitton, Franck Muller) and go to the same vacation spots (St. Bart's, Monaco, Maldives).

The rich will become less and less attached to their own countries and more like global citizens of Richistan. They will invest around the world, rather than putting all their money back into their own communities or countries. They will think, live and buy as Richistanis, not as Americans, Indians or Russians.

Consider the Santo Domingo family from Colombia. As the beer kings of Andean Latin America, the family spent decades plowing their profits back into their business and building up breweries in Colombia, Peru, Ecuador and Panama. In 2005, the brewing giant merged with SAB Miller in return for $7.8 billion in stock, giving the Santo Domingo family its long-awaited "liquidity event."

The family's wealth still relies heavily on the beer business, since they hold the SAB stock. And they still have major businesses in Colombia. But rather than being exposed to the economies of Latin America, the family's beer earnings are now spread throughout North America, Europe and Asia. The Santo Domingos are also investing in U.S. hedge funds, European stocks and Asian funds.

Two family members now live in the United States and are American citizens, and another sibling lives in Europe.

"The family feels that, like any investor, they should be global in their perspective," says Bob Hamshaw, who runs the family's investments from New York. "The SAB Miller merger made them global investors overnight, therefore they have to consider the global economy, not just the local economy or the beer economy. I think you'll see more and more families take this approach around the world."

Just as globalization, capital and technology have made life more competitive for average Americans, they will also make life tougher for Richistanis. The richest Richistanis will be in the best position to take advantage of the global economy; a billionaire, for instance, has the contacts and cash available to, say, buy a hotel in India or invest in a hedge fund in Hong Kong. While everyday investors can also invest overseas, most of their assets will still be in their home countries.

"If I'm worth $3 million, and you're worth $1 billion, it's a lot easier for you to put a few million into a venture-capital fund in India, and that will deliver the better returns," Martiros says. "Those with lower wealth will eventually get done in by consumption. They're simply spending too much to be able to invest significant amounts overseas."

Upper Richistanis will have a bigger lifeboat in the increasingly roiling global economy, while the Lower Richistanis will be less protected.

"The people with very large wealth will become further separated from everyone else," Martiros says.

A Sliver of Hope

The downside of Richistan's future is that inequality will only grow. There will be more Richistanis with ever-bigger yachts; and more people like homeless mother Pertrenia Craig, left adrift in the world's economic storms.

There is, however, one glimmer of hope. Even as the economy and global markets dump more and more money into the hands of a few (or few million), the Richistanis will have even more wealth and power to fix society's most pressing problems. If we accept that the rich aren't the cause of the current inequities, but merely the lucky beneficiaries, we can also hope that they will use their wealth to help target society's deepest problems.

During the Gilded Age and Roaring Twenties, it was the rich, progressive politicians, like the Roosevelts, who took the strongest initiative to shrink the wealth gap in America. The same may prove true during the Third Wave, as Richistani politicians like Jared Polis and Michael Bloomberg use their money to reform the education and health-care systems to better support the middle and lower classes.

And just as wealth will become more global, so will philanthropy. Richistanis will turn their attention not just to fixing New York's inner-city schools and building homes in New Orleans, but also to feeding the hungry in Africa, Cambodia and Brazil. More and more Richistanis can follow the example of Philip Berber, the Irish Jewish Texan who's trying to ease poverty in Ethiopia.

"My hope is that as we become wealthier, and more global in our minds, our hearts will follow," says Berber.

Thus, Richistanis can finally realize Andrew Carnegie's dream for the rich. Someday, the rich will move beyond the excesses of 500-foot yachts, $350,000 Rolls-Royces and alligator-skin jet potties. They will see that their money is not a gift but a responsibility. Through smarter philanthropy like Berber's, Richistanis can eventually fulfill

Carnegie's 100-year-old dream of a "reconciliation between rich and poor, a reign of harmony."

"We shall have an ideal state," he said, "in which the surplus wealth of the few can be made a much more potent force for the elevation of our race."

We can only hope.

Notes

Quotes or facts not attributed to outside sources came from interviews by the author.

INTRODUCTION

3: BY 2004 "Income Inequality in the United States, 1913–1998" Emmanuel Saez and Thomas Piketty, *Quarterly Journal of Economics,* 118(1), 2003, 1–39. Updated with 2004 statistics.

6: WHEN THE FIRST FORBES 400 "The March of the Forbes 400," William P. Barrett, *Forbes,* Sept. 30, 2002.

THE NUMBER OF BILLIONAIRES "Two Decades of Wealth," *Forbes* Web site.

BY 2000 "Currents and Undercurrents: Changes in the Distribution of Wealth, 1989–2004," Arthur B. Kennickell, Senior Economist Federal Reserve Surveys.

PARIS HILTON Sources of Wealth Survey, Prince & Assoc.

7: LOWER RICHISTAN IS THE Federal Reserve Surveys of Consumer Finance, 2004.

8: MORE THAN HALF Ultra High Net Worth Sources of Wealth, Spectrem Group, 2005.

8–9: A MAJORITY Election Survey, Prince & Assoc., 2004.

9: THE ECONOMIC DISTANCE "Currents and Undercurrents,"
Kennickell.

THE AVERAGE INCOME "Income Inequality in the United
States, 1913–1998," Emmanuel Saez and Thomas Piketty,
Quarterly Journal of Economics 118(1), 2003, 1–39; longer
updated version, November 2004, forthcoming in A. B.
Atkinson and T. Piketty, eds., Oxford University Press.

IN 2004 2005 World Wealth Report, Capgemini, Merrill
Lynch, p. 16.

LOWER RICHISTANIS HAVE 2004 Federal Reserve Surveys
of Consumer Finance.

ABOUT 20 PERCENT OF LOWER "Currents and Undercurrents," Kennickell.

IN THE WORDS *The Gospel of Wealth,* Andrew Carnegie,
Commemorative Edition, Carnegie Corporation of New
York, 2001, p. 18.

10: MIDDLE RICHISTAN HAS Ultra High Net Worth Sources of
Wealth, Spectrem.

MOST MIDDLE Election Survey, Prince & Assoc., 2004.

THE INFLATION RATE 2005 World Wealth Report, p. 16.

11: MOST MADE Sources of Wealth Survey, Spectrem, 2005.

12: THE TOTAL WEALTH "Currents and Undercurrents,"
Kennickell.

2

38: "IN AN AGE" *Wealth and Democracy: A Political History of the
American Rich,* Kevin Phillips, Broadway Books, 2002, p. 156.

GOVERNMENT ENCOURAGED Phillips, p. 306.

THE NUMBER OF MILLIONAIRES Phillips, p. 39.

BY 1890 Phillips, p. 43.

THE NUMBER OF MILLIONAIRES Phillips, p. 63.

39: THE SHARE Phillips, p. 76.

THE MIDDLE CLASS ETHOS . . . Phillips, p. 76.

THE SHARE OF WEALTH "Currents and Undercurrents,"
Tables 11A and 11B.

40: HALF OF AMERICA'S Federal Reserve Surveys of Consumer Finances.

FOR THE FIRST TIME 2005 World Wealth Report.

IN 2005 2006 World Wealth Report.

41: YEARS OF LOW INTEREST RATES "Beijing Must Force Radical Reform of State-Owned Firms' Finances," Tom Holland, *South China Morning Post,* July 24, 2006, p. 2.

IN THE SAME PERIOD "Awash in Cash: Cheap Money, Growing Risks," Greg Ip and Mark Whitehouse, *The Wall Street Journal,* Nov. 3, 2005, p. 1.

42: THERE ARE NOW "Despite Blue-Chip Gains, Hedge Funds Increasingly Are Faltering and Closing," Anita Raghavan, Ianthe Jeanne Dugan, and Gregory Zuckerman, *The Wall Street Journal,* October 4, 2006, p. C1.

MORE THAN 4,000 Data from Thomson Financial.

43: "I STARTED AGGRESSIVELY . . ." "Searching for a Home in Atherton," Pui Wing Tam and Mylene Mangalindan, *The Wall Street Journal,* July 12, 2005, p. 1.

DRIVEN BY Data from Thomson Financial.

WALL STREET BANKS Data from The Securities Industry Association.

45: IN THE SAN FRANCISCO "Top 100 Bay Area Executives by Compensation," Todd Wallack, *San Francisco Chronicle,* May 21, 2006, p. F1.

THE RANKS Sources of Wealth Survey, Prince & Assoc.

INHERITED WEALTH ALSO STARTS Sources of Wealth Survey, Prince & Assoc.

48: THE TOP FEDERAL IRS, U.S. Individual Income Tax Rates 1913 to 2005.

50: TO GET INTO Surveys of Consumer Finance, 2004.

3

60: PAUL LAUFER "Ceramics Dynamics," Sally Apgar, *Star-Tribune Newspaper of the Twin Cities,* December 22, 1995.

5

84: AMERICAN MILLIONAIRES 2002 World Wealth Report.
OF THE 400 "A Rolling Tide: Changes in the Distribution
of Wealth in the U.S. 1989–2001," Arthur Kennickell, Fed-
eral Reserve Board, Department of Research and Statistics,
Nov. 2003, p. 3.
THE 2005 FORBES "Dropouts," *Forbes,* Sept 20, 2005.
BILL GATES LOST "Microsoft Guilty of Violating Anti-Trust
Rules," CBS News, April 4, 2000.

85: "WHILE A LARGE . . ." Is This a Great Country? Upward
Mobility and the Chance for Riches in America," Thomas
DiPrete, Columbia University, 2004, p. 11.

6

99: FIREMAN MAINTAINS "Rich vs. Richer: In Palm Beach, the
Old Money Isn't Having a Ball," Robert Frank, *Wall Street
Journal,* May 20, 2005.

104: IN ANCIENT GREECE Quotes and citations related to
ancient Greece were first brought to my attention by Profes-
sor Josiah Ober of Stanford University.
HE WRITES *The Economic and Social Growth of Early Greece,*
Chester G. Starr, Oxford University Press, 1977, pp. 127–28.
"THERE IS A DIFFERENCE . . ." *Aristotle on Rhetoric,*
Book 2, chapter 16, translation by George A. Kennedy,
Oxford University Press, 1991.

105: CORNELIUS "COMMODORE" VANDERBILT Phillips, p. 29.

106: LONGTIME GREENWICHERS "Land of the Big Puts 'Too Big'
to the Test," Alison Leigh Cowan, *The New York Times,*
March 13, 2006.

107: AMONG THE NATION'S Data from Edward Wolff.
ONLY A THIRD "Currents and Undercurrents," Kennickell,
p. 23.

109: IT'S ALSO KNOWN *The Season: Inside Palm Beach and*

America's Richest Society, Ronald Kessler, HarperCollins, 1999, p. 45.

116: PUFF DADDY "Anchor Away: TV5's Dunn to Step Down," Thom Smith, *Palm Beach Post,* April 27, 1998.

7

122: ACCORDING TO ONE STUDY Harrison Group Study cited in "The Trust Equation," *Argent.* Italy figure from *The Economist's* World in Figures 2005.

THE INFLATION RATE 2005 World Wealth Report.

123: "THE BASIS . . ." *The Theory of the Leisure Class,* Thorstein Veblen, Dover Publications, Dover Thrift Editions, 1994, p. 52.

125: YET BOTH BOATS "Top 100 World's Largest Motoryachts," *Yacht Magazine,* July 2006.

ORDERS FOR *Showboat Magazine,* 2006 Global Order Book.

127: "SAIL IS STILL FAR . . ." *Class: A Guide Through the American Status System,* Paul Fussell, Simon & Schuster, 1983, pp. 112–13.

128: GUESTS ABOARD "The World's Hundred Largest Yachts, 2005," Power & Motoryacht Web site.

THE 265-FOOT Power and Motoryacht.

THE SHIP Sourced from yacht builders and a broker.

A SHORT TIME LATER Sourced from yacht builders.

129: A PROFILE OF ELLISON "Absolutely Excessive," Matthew Symonds, *Vanity Fair,* Oct. 2005, p. 318.

"WELL, I DO . . ." Symonds.

130: THE GRANDEST Biltmore Estate Web site.

130–31: THESE HOMES National Association of Home Builders.

131: PEOPLESOFT "A Man's Home May Be His Castle, but Only to a Point," Patricia Leigh Brown, *The New York Times,* Dec. 23, 2005.

EVEN THE ZAMBONI "Greenwich's Outrageous Fortune," Nina Munk, *Vanity Fair,* July 2006, p. 135.

A HOME BUILT "$65 Million Priced to Sell," Amir Afrati, *The Wall Street Journal,* Jan. 13, 2006.

A 60,000-SQUARE-FOOT Afrati, *The Wall Street Journal.*

132: ON THE WEST SIDE Afrati, *The Wall Street Journal.*

THE HOME'S STAIRCASE "Home of Tommy Hilfiger Co-founder on Market," *Inman Real Estate News,* Aug. 7, 2006.

THE NEW RECORD BREAKER "For Sale: Prince's Palace, Aspen ZIP—$135 Million," Troy Hooper, *Rocky Mountain News,* July 12, 2006.

133: GOOGLE FOUNDERS "Wide Flying Moguls," Kevin Delaney, J. Lynn Lunsford, and Mark Maremont, *The Wall Street Journal,* Nov. 4, 2005.

134: AMONG OTHER AMENITIES "Wide Flying Moguls," *The Wall Street Journal.*

"PART OF THE EQUATION . . ." "Wide Flying Moguls," *The Wall Street Journal.*

135: ON ONE DAY IN JANUARY "My Other Vehicle Is a Gulfstream," Guy Trebay, *The New York Times,* Aug. 6, 2006.

139: THE BIG AUCTIONS "Portrait of a Bull Market," Jeanne McDowell, *Time,* Nov. 20, 2006, p. 64.

140: STEVEN COHEN HAS "The Hedge-Fund King Is Getting Nervous," Susan Pulliam, *The Wall Street Journal,* Sept. 16, 2006.

143: SWISS WATCH EXPORTS Federation of the Swiss Watch Industry.

144: OR, AS A *BUSINESSWEEK* "Executive Life: Watches Who Cares What Time It Is?" Bruce Nussbaum, *BusinessWeek,* May 22, 2006.

148: THE FINANCIAL COLUMNIST "Don't Hate Them Because They're Rich," Daniel Gross, *New York Magazine,* Dec. 5, 2005.

151: IN PLUTONOMIES "The Global Investigator: Plutonomy: Buying Luxury, Explaining Global Imbalances," Ajay Kapur et al., Citigroup Equity Research, Oct. 14, 2005, p. 11.

153: THE NATION'S RICHEST Surveys of Consumer Finance 2004.

IN A SERIES OF E-MAILS "Inside Look at a Billionaire's

Budget / Larry Ellison's Spending Worries His Accountant,"
Carrie Kirby, *The San Francisco Chronicle,* Jan. 31, 2006.

154: "THE REAL SIGNIFICANCE . . ." *Luxury Fever: Money and Happiness in an Age of Excess,* by Robert H. Frank, Princeton University Press, 1999, p. 11.

155: "THESE NEW HIGHER . . ." *Luxury Fever,* Frank, p. 276.

8

162: TOTAL CHARITABLE GIVING Giving USA Survey, 2005.
THE NUMBER Giving USA.
BILL GATES'S "Survey of Wealth and Philanthropy,"
The Economist, Feb. 25, 2005.

163: IN 2003 "Nonprofit Efficiency—Fixing the Leak: America's Charities Could Save Billions—and Donors Are Demanding It," Aline Sullivan, *Barron's,* Dec. 8, 2003.

164: IN A 2005 Boston College Center on Wealth and Philanthropy.
"PEOPLE REALIZE . . ." "The Great Giveaway—Like Warren Buffett, a New Wave of Philanthropists Are Rushing to Spend Their Money Before They Die," John Hechinger and Daniel Golden, *The Wall Street Journal,* July 8, 2006.
"THE JOB . . ." Ashoka Web site.

166: THE $1 BILLION FOUNDATION "Philanthropy Google's Way: Not the Usual," Katie Hafner, *The New York Times,* Sept. 14, 2006.
"AFTER A FEW YEARS . . ." "The Birth of Philanthrocapitalism," *The Economist,* Feb. 25, 2006.
"UNTIL YOU START . . ." "The New Face of Philanthropy," John A. Byrne with Julia Cosgrove, Brian Hindo, and Adam Dayan, *BusinessWeek,* Dec. 2, 2002.

9

182: MORE SURPRISINGLY Data from The Colorado Legislative Council.

184: ROUNDING OUT THE GROUP "Gang of Four," Stuart Steers, *5280,* May 2005.

AS BRIDGES TOLD "Gang of Four," Steers.

185: THESE "LEARJET LIBERALS" "Are You a Learjet Liberal?," Jonathan Rauch, *National Journal,* Feb. 10, 2001.

THE NUMBER OF CANDIDATES Jennifer A. Steen, Associate Professor, Boston College.

186: MICHAEL BLOOMBERG "For Bloomberg, 'It's Good to Be a Billionaire,'" Michael Powell and Chris Cillizza, *Washington Post,* Dec. 6, 2005.

188: MORE THAN A DOZEN "Erosion of Estate Tax Is a Lesson in Politics," Jonathan Weisman, *Washington Post,* April 13, 2005.

"THE ESSENCE . . ." *Wealth and Democracy,* Phillips, p. xv.

194: POLIS SAYS "State Ed Board Member Polis Announces He's Gay," Sara Burnett and Stuart Seers, *Rocky Mountain News,* July 6, 2006.

HE SHIPPED 63 "New Name, Flowers Pave Way for Polis," Peter Blake, *Rocky Mountain News,* May 17, 2000.

196: ALSO ONBOARD Forbes 2006 400 Richest Americans.

200: DYER WAS LATER "Flap over $10 House," Peggy Lowe, *Rocky Mountain News,* Sept. 16, 2004.

201: "THEY ALL CAME TOGETHER . . ." "Their Contributions Helped Buy a Cadillac Campaign in Colo.," Josh Kurtz, *Roll Call,* Feb. 2, 2005.

10

204: AS WE SAW IN THE FIRST PNC Advisors, Wealth and Values Survey, Jan. 20, 2005.

IN HIS BOOK *The Virtue of Prosperity: Finding Values in an Age of Techno-Affluence,* Dinesh D'Souza, Simon & Schuster, 2000, p. 107.

11

221: BASED ON AVERAGE FAMILY Survey of Consumer Finance 2004.

UP TO $15 TRILLION "Over the Next 50 Years Trillions Will Be Passed On," Jeff Gammage, *Philadelphia Inquirer,* March 6, 2004.

A SURVEY BY PRINCE "Who Gets the Money," Prince & Assoc., 2006.

TODAY'S RICH "The Status of Wealth in America," Worth-Harrison Taylor Study, *Worth Magazine,* Nov. 2005, p. 31.

222: PRIVATE SCHOOLS "Getting over the Wall," Wendy Belzberg, *New York Sun,* Feb. 13, 2003.

227: IN ONE STUDY PNC Advisors, Wealth and Values Survey, 2005.

12

240: "VIRTUALLY NONE . . ." "Displaced in 'Crisis' of Affordable Housing," Matthew Haggman, *The Miami Herald,* Nov. 3, 2005.

"I'M ABOUT TO CRY . . ." "Helpless and Homeless," Tonya Alanez, Lisa J. Huriash, and Jamie Malrenee, *South Florida Sun-Sentinel,* Nov. 4, 2005.

241: "WE FELT BADLY . . ." "Full Speed Ahead," Amy Martinez, *The Miami Herald,* Nov. 3, 2005.

242: "YOU COULD COME . . ." "Full Speed Ahead."

MEDIAN INCOMES Economic Policy Institute.

THE RICHEST 1 PERCENT Federal Reserve Surveys of Consumer Finance.

THE SHARE OF NATIONAL INCOME "Income Inequality in the United States, 1913–1998," with Thomas Piketty, *Quarterly Journal of Economics,* 118(1), 2003, 1–39 (tables and figures updated to 2004).

243: VOTER APATHY *Inequality Matters: The Growing Divide in*

America and Its Poisonous Consequences, James Lardner and David A. Smith, eds., The New Press, 2005, p. 22.

"AS INCOMES CONTINUE . . ." *Falling Behind: How Rising Inequality Harms the Middle Class,* Robert H. Frank, University of California Press, 2007.

245: EXPERTS PREDICT World Wealth Report 2006.

249: THROUGH SMARTER *The Gospel of Wealth,* Carnegie, p. 21.

250: "WE SHALL HAVE AN IDEAL . . ." *The Gospel of Wealth,* p. 21.

Acknowledgments

This book would not have been possible without the support of countless editors, colleagues, friends, family and wealth experts.

I am grateful to Paul Steiger and Dan Hertzberg of *The Wall Street Journal* for giving me the time and resources to create the wealth beat and expand my reporting into a book. They are two of the most caring, meticulous and dedicated editors in journalism and I'm proud to have worked for them for the past 13 years.

Thanks also to *Journal* editors Dave Kansas, Ellen Pollock and Mike Miller for their editing expertise and their dedication to long-form, narrative journalism.

Ken Wells, author, beer expert and editor extraordinaire, helped conceptualize Richistan over a few cold ones at Foxhounds. He worked tirelessly as my agent, adviser and proposal editor to make the book happen. John Mahaney and Annik LaFarge (now at Bloomsbury) helped refine my ideas into a cohesive book and kept me on deadline (almost).

More than 100 wealthy individuals gave me the one thing their money can't buy: their time. Ed Bazinet, Tim and Edra Blixseth, Pete and Hilary Musser, George Cloutier and Tiffany Spadafora, Frank Butler, Ron Perelman, Chris Taylor, Philip and Donna Berber, Jared Polis, Tim Gill, Kyle Circle and the "kids" from IFF were among those kind enough to entrust me with their stories. I hope I have represented them fairly and accurately.

Thanks also to Mary Starkey for letting me into Butler Boot Camp for two weeks, Michael Sonnenfeldt for allowing me to attend a Tiger 21 meeting, and Doug Freeman and Lee Hausner for letting me come to one of their wealth-education seminars.

Arthur Kennickell and Gerhard Fries of the Federal Reserve helped me crunch the numbers on the millionaire populations, and Russ Alan Prince and Spectrem provided me with their copious research.

Larry Ingrassia and Adam Bryant have been loyal friends, mentors and advisers throughout my career, even after they went to work for "the competition." They inspire me every day to be a better reporter and storyteller. James H. Ottaway Jr. has helped teach me the value of persistence and perspective in journalism, and I will miss his presence at Dow Jones.

Eric Anderson, a true journalist at heart, was my guide to all things Colorado and made several improvements to the manuscript. Ken Brown also spent hours poring over my first draft and giving me his expert edit.

Stephen Martiros taught me about the economics of wealth and global capital flows in a way that even *I* could understand (and if I didn't, it's not his fault). Thanks also to Laird Pendleton for his insights into wealth-peering and the history of wealth.

To all my friends who have tolerated my absence for the past year, I hope I can make it up to you. I am especially grateful to Perk and Marguerite Hixon for their generosity, wisdom and keen insights into the changing character of wealth. They have shown me the true meaning of what Edmund Burke called "the unbought grace of life."

Most of all, I'd like to thank my family—Mom, Dad, Kathi, Natia, Betty, and all the extended clan, for their support over the years.

The person who worked hardest on this book (other than me) is my wife, Rebecca. Over the past year, she has kept our lives together, sacrificed countless weekends and family vacations and taken care of our daughter—all while holding down one of the most demanding jobs in the world. This book is truly for her.

Finally, thanks to little Amelia, whose smiles at the end of every day made me feel like the richest man on earth.

Index

About the Author

ROBERT FRANK is a senior special writer at *The Wall Street Journal,* where he writes a weekly column and daily blog called The Wealth Report. He has been with *The Journal* for 13 years, with postings in Atlanta, London, Singapore and New York. He was part of a team of reporters that won an Overseas Press Club award in 1998 for its coverage of developing economies.

He lives in New York with his wife and daughter.